The
TREE
in my
GAR
DEN

The
TREE
in my
GAR

Choose one tree, plant it—and change the world

DEN

KATE BRADBURY

Illustrated by LUCILLE CLERC

Contents

Why trees?
Why now?

Our world is on fire. Literally, in parts of California, Europe, and Australia, wildfires are tearing through forests and communities, killing people and wildlife. Metaphorically, too, parts of the world burn so hot, we will soon be unable to live in them. But rather than feeling hopeless, let's join together to plant trees. Starting in our gardens.

Climate change and its associated effects of biodiversity loss and extreme weather events make for grim reading. The sixth assessment report from the Intergovernmental Panel on Climate Change, written in 2022, warns that time is running out to act to avoid catastrophe. Temperatures are rising, rivers are flooding or drying up, and species are dying out. In 2021, more than 400 weather stations broke their heat records, with the highest temperatures in Canada increasing by a whopping 4.6 percent to 121.3°F (49.6°C) and the Pakistan city of Jacobabad logging temperatures of 126°F (52°C). There, the heat and extreme humidity have been deemed too much for the human body to bear.

We're staring down the barrel of mechanical pollination because there are no longer insects to do the job for us; of cloud seeding technologies to make it rain because rain doesn't fall where we need it to; and of not being able to live in vast swathes of Earth due to extremes of heat, humidity, flooding, and wind.

How did we get here?

Well, it all started with deforestation. In the last 6,000 years, we have lost half of the forests in Europe, as space has been taken for agriculture and growing human populations. Deforestation continues today, mostly in tropical regions such as Brazil, where global demand for cheap beef drives competition for land. And now, for the first time, the Amazon rainforest is thought to emit more carbon dioxide than it can absorb due to deforestation and changing weather patterns. Around the world,

we destroy around 25 million acres (10 million hectares) of forest every year, which adds up to an area about the size of Portugal each decade.

It's not just deforestation that causes climate change. Use of fossil fuels, from cars and planes to space rockets; the intensification of agriculture, particularly the global meat and fish industries; and the consumption of peat, along with the mismanagement of peat bogs and moorland, all play their part.

And yet there is hope.

What can we do next?

Some 50 percent of deforestation in the world is offset by regrowing or new forests, which should only increase as global awareness of climate change and deforestation expands. More of us are buying less and recycling more, taking fewer flights and eating less meat. But—and I'm not going to beat around the bush here (pardon the pun)—we're in a difficult situation. We can get out of it, at least in part and depending on how quickly we act, with the help of the things we chopped down in the first place: trees! You could plant one in your garden today.

Trees are only part of the solution to tackling climate change and loss of biodiversity. We need to change the way we treat the world's oceans, our remaining peat bogs, grasslands, and ponds. Carbon is stored in a wide range of habitats, including our gardens, and we need to protect them all. We can (and should) join environmental organizations and wildlife charities, sign petitions, and make better choices when food shopping and at polling stations.

But there's something about tree planting that gives us ownership of the issue—that rewards us for and reminds us of what we've done. We plant a tree, water it, and watch it grow. We marvel at birds landing on its branches and at insects eating its leaves and pollinating its flowers. We might eat its fruit and share it with the wildlife and fall in love with its glorious fall coloring. We might sit beneath it and listen to the rustle of its leaves or put our ear to its trunk to hear the gurgle of rising sap in spring.

Trees are great. They root us to the land and connect us to the seasons. People tell me "it's not spring until my hawthorn flowers" and "not summer until I've eaten my first cherry." At Christmas, we bring trees into our homes and make wreaths with berry-laden branches.

For me, the turning of the seasons is marked by the achingly long days of waiting for the first leaves to unfurl on my garden trees after winter. (I have three: a mountain ash, hawthorn, and silver birch; pp.14–15.)

In planting and observing trees, we notice more and are more mindful as a result. Our blood pressure lowers and our mental health improves. On top of that, trees breathe in carbon dioxide and breathe out oxygen; help support insect, mammal, and bird populations; prevent flooding; stabilize temperatures; and filter wind. Trees are amazing, aren't they? To think we ever chopped them down. To think we're still chopping them down!

Plant a tree

As the old Chinese proverb goes, "The best time to plant a tree was 20 years ago. The second best time is now." By planting a tree, you will directly help reduce some of the effects of climate change. Each drop of water absorbed by the tree's roots is a drop that won't join others to form a puddle or a flood. Each ounce of carbon dioxide taken in by its leaves will reduce the amount floating in the atmosphere. Each bee that visits its flowers will not go hungry, and each egg laid on its leaves will provide food for species further up the food chain.

To plant a tree is to give life to wildlife, to you, and to your children and grandchildren. Planting trees is an act of power and rebellion—a middle finger to a world of greed and corruption. As you lower your tree's roots into the ground and cover them with soil, you become part of a global reforestation movement. Isn't that something?

Trees are amazing. To think we ever chopped them down. To think we're still chopping them down!

Why gardens?

It's estimated that there are around 123 million households in the US, and just over 31 million of us have a garden. If every one of us planted a tree in our gardens tomorrow, that would be 31 million more trees in the US, each one absorbing carbon dioxide while providing food and homes for wildlife, not to mention giving us something nice to look at. 31 million trees. Tomorrow.

How much nectar and pollen would 31 million trees add for our beleaguered bees? How many more leaves would there be for moths to lay their eggs on and caterpillars to eat? How many more baby birds would have bellies full of those caterpillars, plus the aphids, leaf miners, and other bugs that also eat leaves and live among trees? How many more opossums would be able to gather fallen leaves from beneath these trees to line their cozy dens in fall?

Trees are life

Each one is a city, home to hundreds of beings, from the tiniest thrips to the wriggliest caterpillars and the largest birds. In planting one, we might create some much-needed shade in the garden—a focal point, maybe, as something to sit under as our feet poke out into the sun. But in doing so, we create something so much more wonderful. We provide somewhere for a bird to land as it checks out our feeders or bird box. We provide a trunk for a squirrel to shimmy up, in hot pursuit of another squirrel, in spring. We provide flowers for bees, leaves for caterpillars, and berries for birds. We provide little nooks and crannies in the bark where a queen wasp might take shelter over winter. We provide a view through a window, from which we might marvel at spring blossom, fall leaf color, or nesting birds. Something that connects us to the outside, no matter what time of year it is, through which we can measure the passage of time.

And as each day passes, as each bird lands on a branch and each caterpillar munches a leaf, that tree in your garden is absorbing carbon dioxide. One tree in one garden. It probably won't make much difference, will it? But 31 million trees? Why, that's a forest.

Creating a network

Combined, our 31 million gardens have the potential to become a wildlife reserve in their own right. Knitted together via holes in or beneath fences and gates, they comprise a network of habitats the length and breadth of the country. Gardens mimic habitats we call the "woodland edge," where shrubs and small trees grow among grasses and wildflowers. The wildlife we attract to our gardens reflects that—the birds, amphibians, bees, and butterflies that visit are all creatures of the woodland edge. So our gardens are predestined for tree planting—trees belong in our gardens, no matter how big or small they are.

You might see the space outside your front or back door as small and meaningless, but with a few choice plants, it can act as a stepping stone from one habitat to the next. What's a stepping stone, you ask? Imagine a long, gray road bookended by green spaces, with the wildlife in each space cut off from the other because the long, gray road between them is too long and too gray—there's no shelter or food to help them on their journey. Add a few gardens and suddenly the wildlife can move—bees and butterflies can drink nectar to give them energy to fly, and frogs and rabbits can hide beneath a hedge or shrub. These stepping-stone habitats are crucial in the fight against climate change and biodiversity loss because they allow wildlife to move around—that is, they connect habitats, enabling wildlife to find more suitable habitats if they need to. Studies have shown that some insect species are already moving north, in search of cooler temperatures. If there are too many long, gray roads on their journey, they're not going to survive.

Choosing the right tree

The space outside your front or back door, then, has the potential to save lives and promote biodiversity. You just need to plant it up. Tree planting can seem daunting at first. You may be anxious about your tree growing too big, casting too much shade or shedding too many leaves. And what will the neighbors say if you reduce the light to their garden? These are all valid points, which is why it's vital to take your time when choosing the tree in your garden (see pp.52–143). The right tree will bring you years of enjoyment, wildlife watching, and a feeling of having done something "good." The wrong tree will lead to years of anxiety, after which you or someone else who inherits the space will have to chop it down.

Before you plant your tree, think about what you want from it. How tall will it grow in your lifetime? How wide or dense will its canopy be? If you need privacy, you could plant a tree with a dense canopy, such as an ornamental pear; if you prefer filtered light, then go for something like a silver birch, with its airy canopy, thin branches, and small leaves. For the best wildlife options, it's a good idea to choose native trees (see pp.20–21), as these have evolved with the species you want to protect. To take account of climate change, you might consider a tree from a more southerly region, as global heating could mean it survives better in 50 years' time. Do you want fruit or berries (see pp.40–41)? Fall color (see pp.42-43) or year-round interest? Some trees really have it all.

This book offers information about a lot of trees, which you can compare and contrast before making your big planting decision. You'll also find lots of reasons why you should plant trees because I want to hammer home how important and joyful they are. I hope, in reading this book, you will be armed with all the knowledge you need to plant and care for your garden tree. I also hope we can reforest the planet, one garden at a time.

One tree in one garden. It probably won't make much difference, will it? But 31 million trees? Why, that's a forest.

The trees
in my garden

*I moved into my house in January 2019. A Victorian
terrace, it has a narrow, 40ft (12m) garden that backs on
to other houses and, beyond it, a park. I had high hopes
for lots of wildlife. But the garden was planted with things
that held little value for them: a huge Japanese spindle, a
common jasmine, and a eucalyptus tree that was planted
far too close to the house. I set to work immediately.*

Wishing to start from a blank canvas, I dug up everything. I kept what was useful and donated the rest to friends and neighbors. And then I started again from scratch.

My trees
I planted the trees first: a gorgeous mountain ash (*Sorbus aucuparia*), a Midland hawthorn (*Crataegus laevigata*), and a silver birch (*Betula pendula*). They instantly gave shape to the garden and provided me with a window into a world I hadn't finished creating. I planted them when they were dormant and I still remember my excitement as the first leaf buds burst in spring—the freshest green on twigs that had been bare for so long.

What followed has been endlessly delightful. I marveled at the first birds that landed in the trees as they navigated around the newly designed space. I listened and watched as the first bees found the first flowers and laughed as the first blackbirds found the first berries. Imagine my joy when I kicked my first pile of fallen leaves. I fell in love with my trees as soon as I planted them, and my love for them grows as well as they do.

Mountain ash
At the back of the garden is the mountain ash. I chose it because it won't grow too big and it has gorgeous flat plates of spring blossom, followed by fat red berries. I love watching its mittenlike buds form in late winter and burst into beautiful pinnate leaves. Many pollinators use its flowers, while blackbirds and robins eat its berries. Other species visit for shelter—everything from squirrels to starlings.

Hawthorn

Ten feet (3m) from the mountain ash is the hawthorn, a slightly smaller tree that shouldn't outgrow the garden. The space between them is enough for their roots to exchange food and information, and one day I hope their canopies will meet, too. It has single white blossoms loved by bees, then dark red "haws" that birds rely upon in fall. Its leaves are popular with many moths, which I hope will use the tree for breeding when it's more mature. Its twiggy frame will make the perfect spot for birds to nest, too.

Silver birch

On the other side is the silver birch, the tallest tree in the garden but the shortest-lived. I love its heart-shaped leaves that have been found by leaf miners and buff-tip caterpillars and its beautiful, peeling bark. I planted it because I wanted to watch blue tits hang upside down from its slender branches and pick at its catkins. Watching them do this fills my heart on even the darkest winter days. In November, it's the most gorgeous thing for miles; its leaves turn yellow before falling into a satisfying pile.

Making room for more trees

If I had a bigger garden, I'd plant more—I'd have my own arboretum if I could. Instead, I make do with smaller specimens: a tiny mixed hedge of hawthorn, hazel, field rose, and common buckthorn. Then there are two much smaller trees: a Kilmarnock willow and a strawberry tree. The willow is at its maximum height and sits at the edge of my pond, and the strawberry tree is in a pot in which it will grow some more before I find space for it in the garden.

I love watching the mountain ash's mittenlike buds form in late winter and burst into beautiful pinnate leaves.

UNDERSTANDING
TREES

Having evolved over millennia, trees are the foundations for so much life on Earth. It's easy to say that we need to plant more trees, but if we want to make a more meaningful difference, knowing which varieties to plant—and where—is crucial. By getting to know trees before you plant, you'll be able to reap more rewards later on.

Trees over time

Trees have been growing on Earth for around 400 million years. Some of the earliest species can still be seen in gardens today, including the monkey puzzle tree (Araucaria araucana) *and the maidenhair tree* (Ginkgo biloba); *they evolved around 248 million years ago, which is why they're sometimes known as living fossils.*

Over the millennia, the shape of trees, the way they absorb water and nutrients, and how they reproduce have all evolved to ensure trees are as successful as they can be in their given environment. Each tree's leaf shape, bark, flowers, fruit, and seeds are the way they are for very specific reasons.

Trees have adapted to grow in wet or dry soils, up mountains or in valleys, in rainforests and cloud forests—every environment has a set of perfectly adapted trees that grow successfully in it. Most trees thrive in a community growing alongside others, but some do best growing on their own. The black walnut tree, for example, secretes a chemical called juglone from its roots, which can inhibit the growth of nearby plants.

Tree shape
Trees have evolved their shape to make the most of available light levels. The crown of broadleaf trees (such as oak) is large and rounded so their leaves can absorb light in cloudy, temperate environments. Conifers, typically from colder climates, tend to be cone-shaped, as this helps them absorb light when the sun is low on the horizon (resulting in weaker rays). Cone-shaped trees are also able to shed snow easily.

Leaf shape and size
Leaf shape is determined by the need to absorb light and carbon dioxide, but other factors—such as climate, temperature, day length, water availability, nutrition, and predators—influence shape, too. Large leaves absorb more light than smaller ones

but lose moisture via evaporation and can scorch in too much sun. Evergreen trees have leaves that are shaped to minimize evaporation. To prevent water loss, leaves may be tiny, needlelike, waxy, glossy, lobed, or toothed.

Protection from predators

The outer bark protects a tree from disease and damage—many species, including oaks and willows, have bark containing tannins unpalatable to mammals. The bark helps the tree retain moisture and protects living cells from infections from bacteria, fungi, and other pathogens. Some trees also grow thorns to protect leaves and seeds from being eaten.

Flowers, fruit, nuts, and seeds

Each stage of a tree's reproductive cycle has evolved to suit its local climate and pollinating wildlife. Tree flowers have evolved to be pollinated by wind or insects (see pp.40–41) in order to produce fruit. Most fruits have evolved to be eaten by birds or mammals, which then pass the seeds of the fruit through their digestive system and disperse them elsewhere. Winged seeds such as those of sycamore are carried on the wind. Other trees have evolved more interesting ways to reproduce. The crack willow is so called because of the loud cracking noise its branches make when they fall off the tree and into water below, in which they are carried downstream, sometimes rooting into a new area of riverbank.

Trees today

Today, trees still grow in their native environments (see pp.20–21), but human intervention has also seen them growing in locations you wouldn't otherwise find them. Victorian plant hunters paved the way for trees to be grown in regions far from their origins, bringing back seeds of trees such as Chinese magnolia and giant redwood from California. Most of the ornamental trees we grow in our gardens today are not native: Himalayan birch, Japanese maple, Australian eucalyptus, and Turkey oak are examples that all hail from regions beyond our own.

What's more, plant breeders have crossed closely related trees to create hybrids. These trees may be crossed to improve resistance to disease; grow taller or shorter; have a more ornamental growth habit, such as weeping branches; or bear more flowers or fruit.

Native or non-native?

A native tree is generally considered to be one that has grown in a given place since the last Ice Age, and is therefore perfectly adapted to the climate it lives in. But today's climate is changing too quickly for many trees to evolve and adapt in time to the new conditions. Should we therefore be looking to non-natives to grow in their place?

In the US, trees colonized the land after the glaciers melted, slowly moving from areas that remained free of ice into areas that had previously been covered in glaciers. As such, they have evolved closely with the wildlife that have also colonized the land after the ice retreated. Native trees and other plants are therefore considered to be better for wildlife than non-natives.

Simply put, they already have relationships in place: they flower when pollinators need flowers and bear berries and seeds when birds need those berries and seeds. Moths lay eggs on the leaves of (often specific) native trees at exactly the right time for their caterpillars to be the perfect size for baby birds to digest. Native trees, plants,

and their corresponding wildlife grow together as part of a series of complex ecosystems that have evolved over the last 11,500 years— and as a wildlife gardener, I do everything I can in order to cram as many native species into my garden as possible.

But the truth is, native trees are struggling. Native trees—and indeed all native plants—are under a variety of stresses. Pollution, deforestation, agricultural runoff, and the ongoing effects of climate change are all taking their toll. To give one example: as the climate warms, pests and diseases are moving north. This is resulting in an invasion of areas that were once free of such problems and adding to the stresses felt by native trees.

Matching trees with climate

The United States is a vast area with multiple climate zones differing not only in mean annual temperature extremes, but also in soil type, daylength during summer, rainfall, and a host of other factors. As climate change brings warmer temperatures—and often wetter or drier rainfall patterns—to the various ecoregions of the US, the performance of both native and non-native species in our gardens will inevitably be affected. This may mean that plants once commonly grown in the Deep South potentially become appropriate for regions farther north—say, in Kentucky. Wide-ranging native trees may have "ecotypes" that are adapted to local conditions. Growing ecotypes from a region farther south may be one way to bring native plants into new garden situations.

Human-made hybrids could also work, where closely related trees are crossed to introduce natural resilience to both climate change and diseases. This technique has worked before: *Ulmus* 'New Horizon' is a hybrid of Japanese and Siberian elms. It's completely resistant to Dutch Elm disease, introduced to Britain from Canada in the 1960s, which wiped out most of the elms. Being so closely related to our native elms, could the wildlife that use elms, such as the white letter hairstreak butterfly, be tempted by these new hybrids, and so have a better chance of survival?

The way forward

It seems to me that the most sensible route in US gardens is to plant a mix of natives and carefully selected non-natives. We need native trees now for our native wildlife now. Planting more native trees will create corridors through which native wildlife can travel, especially as they will need to move north as temperatures increase. But we also need to plant trees now that will cope better with the increased temperatures and humidity of the future. And that's where non-natives come in. But we must choose non-natives that support biodiversity to enable better adaptations to our changing climate and, ultimately, more survival.

Trees
and fungi

Fungi get bad press in gardens, which is sad, because they mostly do a lot of good. Fungi are essential for the growth and health of garden trees. The mushrooms or toadstools we see above the soil's surface are the fruiting bodies, a tiny part of the main body of the fungus whose stringlike fungal threads (hyphae) live below the surface, on or around tree roots in networks known as mycelium.

Many trees depend on fungi to help them grow. In woodlands, miles of hyphae grow underground, connecting tree roots to the soil and enabling them to better take up water and nutrients. These mycorrhizal (fungus–root) partnerships also link the root systems of different trees to each other, creating networks of trees sometimes referred to as the "wood wide web." In some species, such as beech, fungi enable trees to support each other, with healthy trees giving nutrients to less healthy ones. The more we learn about trees, the more we realize they are a community species. So that one tree in your garden could well be connected to the tree next door through a fungal network, with which they exchange nutrients, carbon, and information. In return, the tree provides the fungi with sugars—unlike plants, fungi do not photosynthesize, so they rely on other living bodies to provide them with the energy they need.

Some fungi can protect trees from drought, disease, and predators. Gardeners are forever trying to get rid of fairy rings on lawns, despite the fact that the *Marasmius oreades* fungus responsible feeds the lawn and improves its health. Honey fungus is known only for its tree and shrub-killing properties, but there are several species, some coexisting with trees and shrubs for years. In soils contaminated with heavy metals, fungi can help remove them.

Fungi are amazing and deserve more recognition. Different fungi have different specialisms, so the greater variety of fungi available to your tree, the healthier it will be.

UNDERSTANDING TREES

To plant or not to plant?

As trees grow, they pull in carbon dioxide via their leaves (see p.34) and store it in their trunk, roots, and branches. When they die, that carbon is released slowly back into the atmosphere. Planting trees can, therefore, help slow climate change, as the more trees we plant, the more carbon dioxide is absorbed. But trees alone will not solve climate change, and tree planting can sometimes do more harm than good.

In the US in 2021, 7.3 million trees were planted in national forests, and new trees are being planted in gardens, towns, and rural areas as well. Elsewhere, trees are being planted with even more gusto: the Indian state of Uttar Pradesh claims to have planted 50 million trees in one day. The Great Green Wall of the Sahara and the Sahel is an ambitious international project that involves the planting of trees across the Sahel to prevent the expansion—or desertification—of the Sahara Desert. If you're looking for a good news story, look no further than Costa Rica, which doubled its forest cover in just 30 years.

As citizens of tree-poor countries, we're encouraged to plant trees to help fight climate change, but it's worth pausing for breath before we reach for the spade.

When not to plant trees

The first thing to consider is that not all land was originally forested. As well as woodland, there are grasslands, wetlands, and peat bogs—landscapes where trees don't belong. These complex habitats store carbon in their own right—it's estimated that the world's peat bogs store twice as much carbon as its forests. Grasslands store less carbon than woodlands, but the storage is more reliable—grasslands are less at risk from forest fires, for example, which can quickly release thousands of tons of carbon back into the atmosphere. The carbon storage of our 31 million gardens, with their accumulated plants, trees, lawns, and ponds, shouldn't be sniffed at either.

It goes without saying that, rather than replanting forests, we should be protecting those we already have, from the millions of trees felled in the US for urban expansion, to the Amazon rainforest lost, to cattle ranches in Brazil. Protecting existing woodland is much better for preventing climate change and supporting wildlife than planting new trees, which take time to sequester (store) carbon and offer the habitats of established forests.

Natural regeneration

Another alternative is to let land revert to its original state, with minimum input from us humans. Termed "rewilding," this system could be used instead of mass planting schemes. For example, a study published in 2021 suggests that half of Britain's new forests have been planted not by humans, but by jays, which bury acorns in fall. Along with gray squirrels, jays bury acorns to eat later when food runs low but often forget about them—and a woodland is born.

Letting wildlife replant our forests will have many benefits: no plastic tree guards littering the landscape, no need to water vulnerable saplings, no digging of the soil (which in itself releases carbon). Animals can be brought in to "manage" the habitat, grazing the land gently to allow some species to grow while preventing total reforestation.

Rewilding isn't appropriate for gardens or for our cities and parks, so in these habitats, we must plant trees. But let's do so armed with the knowledge that trees like to grow together; that scrub is an invaluable wildlife habitat; and that, on its own, your one tree is simply not enough to reverse or even slow down the effects of climate change.

Half of Britain's new forests are thought to have been planted by jays, which bury acorns in fall.

Trees
in cities

We already know that trees absorb carbon dioxide, improve well-being, and provide homes for wildlife. But in cities, they have even more benefits—from cooling their surroundings, absorbing polluting particles, and preventing flooding, to reducing crime and road rage (yes, really!). The more trees we plant, the more comfortable and healthy our cities will be to live in, now and in the future.

According to the United Nations, more than 50 percent of people live in cities now, with nearly 70 percent of the world's human population expected to live in cities by 2050. Urban areas are warmer than rural areas because there are more hard, dark surfaces to absorb heat from the sun—every pavement, road, and wall acts as a storage heater. What's more, the structure of some cities—particularly those with narrow streets and tall buildings—prevents heat from being released, as there's little opportunity for natural wind flow. Human activity in cities also contributes to urban heating, with motorized vehicles, buildings, and (ironically) air-conditioning units all creating "waste heat."

This absorption of heat contributes to what's known as the "Heat Island Effect," with some cities already dramatically warmer than their rural counterparts. Warmer cities might not seem so bad now, but a 2019 study predicts a 4°F (2°C) global rise by 2050 will see city temperatures rise exponentially higher. In the hottest months, these temperature increases will not only affect people's ability to work, but will dramatically affect their ability to live well, with those with asthma and heart issues most at risk.

Cooling effects

Trees, and plants generally, are cooler than pavements and walls. If you've ever walked into a woodland on a hot summer's day, you will have felt the immediate relief of the sudden drop in temperature as you entered a world that instantly refreshed you.

Growing more trees and plants will help reduce urban heating, as each tree creates shade and prevents sunlight from hitting hard surfaces. Tree roots will also absorb water and so reduce the risk of flooding, while the leaves will absorb pollution particles and help clean the air. The shade cast by tree canopies provides a break from the heat, while leaves, bark, branches, flowers, and berries provide food and homes for wildlife.

We should all, therefore, be planting trees in every available park, tree pit (a hole made for a street tree), and bit of waste ground across our cities now. We should also be planting ivy and other climbers up walls of buildings and adding green roofs and balcony gardens wherever we can. Remember that, as well as deflecting heat, every single leaf absorbs carbon dioxide and every root holds onto water.

Planting street trees

As lovely as street trees are, the sad truth is that planting them can be complicated and expensive. Street trees usually need to be planted with root barrier systems to prevent their roots from disrupting cables and pipes beneath pavements, which provide electricity, Wi-Fi, and water to businesses and homes. They need to have grates fitted to stop the roots from becoming compacted by city footfall or creating trip hazards on the pavement surface. They need to be planted on wide pavements to ensure full access for those in wheelchairs. Ideally, and sadly, they should not be fruiting (female) trees, as fruit creates a mess, as well as a potential slip hazard, when it falls to the ground. Male trees produce valuable pollen for the pollinators that are around, but the pollen may cause issues for people with hayfever.

What's more, street trees need regular watering to keep them alive (at least in their first couple of years) and pruning to make sure they don't encroach on the road or drop branches. In fall, they need their leaves collected and disposed of.

Do trees like being street trees? Do they enjoy having their roots restricted and not connected to other trees, their canopies pruned into regimented shapes, and their pollen floating around the city with few female flowers to fertilize? I think, on balance, the answer has to be: no. We know trees are communal species. We know they do best when growing together in groups—that they connect to each other and share information and even keep each other alive through the power of their connected root systems, aided by fungi (see p.22). Some studies have also shown that street trees absorb less carbon dioxide than those growing in more natural environments.

I like street trees: they make me happy, and I love a tree-lined street. But given the huge cost of planting and maintaining them, plus the fact that it's probably not the best option for the trees themselves, I think we should look for other ways to "reforest" our cities.

Alternatives to street trees

We could start with planting small copses in parks, where there are fewer, if any, cables and pipes to be mindful of and unrestricted ground where tree roots can connect as they would in the wild. We should look at areas of waste ground and see if groups of trees can be planted there, with small urban forests popping up across our cities.

Existing street trees should be looked after and tree-lined streets celebrated. Empty tree pits, where a street tree once grew, should be replanted, as there will already be no cables or pipes to be mindful of. Maybe city planners and road builders can look at ways we can bring trees to our streets without growing them in such stressful conditions. Instead of tree-lined streets, we can have tree-rich corners, with small groups of trees on areas of bare ground. Maybe we can find spaces for urban hedges and climbers where trees won't grow. We can also, of course, plant trees in urban gardens. There's absolutely nothing stopping us from doing that.

We should be planting trees in every available park, tree pit, and bit of waste urban ground now.

PLANT ONE TREE

A tree is a remarkable thing. From root to branch, through the seasonal cycles of blossom and fruit, to the glorious displays of deciduous fall color, a single tree can transform a garden and captivate us year after year. Find out how these amazing life-cycle stages can be put to use in your garden and make your tree an intrinsic part of it.

Parts of a tree

So far, I've talked about the big picture: the evolution of trees, their community, and their role in rewilding and in our cities. But what, exactly, is a tree? Botanically speaking, it's a woody plant that lives for many years, characterized by its tall (usually single) trunk, bark, and branches. Each tree has evolved independently to compete for sunlight so it can photosynthesize (make its own food using sunlight).

Superficially, trees are made of the roots, trunk, and crown—which includes stems, twigs, and leaves.

Roots

The roots absorb water and nutrients from the soil, store nutrients, and anchor the tree into the earth. Tree roots are typically shallow. They're mostly found in the top 2ft (60cm) of the soil and rarely penetrate deeper than about 6½ft (2m). However, some trees have a taproot (a long, single root that penetrates into the soil) to reach deep for extra sources of water and nutrients.

Tree roots usually spread around two to three times the radius of the tree's canopy. As the tree grows, any taproot recedes in size while the lateral (side) roots thicken and become woody, eventually protruding from the soil. Many trees depend on a symbiotic relationship between their roots and mycorrhizal fungi (see p.22), which aids the absorption of water and nutrients.

Trunk

The trunk comprises several parts, some of which transport food and nutrients. At the center is the heartwood, which is the core of the tree and its strongest part. While it is not technically living, the core will retain its strength as long as the outer layers of the trunk are intact.

Around the heartwood is the sapwood, which contains vascular xylem tissues that transport watery fluid (known as sap, and containing minerals and other nutrients) from the tree's roots to the branches and leaves. As the tree matures, the older

sapwood becomes heartwood. On the outside of the trunk is the woody bark, which protects the inner parts. Only the inner layers of bark are alive, with new bark produced by a vascular system of cells known as the cambium.

The innermost bark layer is called the phloem, and, when young, contains vascular tissues that transport food (glucose) in sap from the leaves to the branches, fruit, trunk, and roots of the tree. As the phloem matures, it turns to cork, giving way to newer material to carry nutrients around the tree.

Crown

The crown of the tree is made up of its branches and leaves. The leaves produce glucose (sugar) via the process of photosynthesis. This involves using energy from the sun, which is absorbed using chlorophyll in each leaf cell; chlorophyll also gives the leaf its green color. The sun's energy is used to split water molecules into their hydrogen and oxygen atoms. The hydrogen is then combined with carbon dioxide to create glucose, which is transported to provide nutrients for other areas of the tree. The oxygen is released back into the atmosphere.

How trees grow

Trees absorb water through their roots and make food in their leaves. They grow by producing new cells, but only in certain parts of the tree, called meristems (unlike animals, where cell production can occur in most parts of the body).

Trees have meristems on their branch tips, root tips, and leaf and flower buds and in the vascular cambium, which produces new phloem and xylem cells each year, particularly in regions with pronounced seasons. This causes the trunk, branches, and roots to increase in diameter seasonally (which is how you can "age" a tree from its "growth rings"). So trees grow outward and upward, but only from their tips and outer edges. Most tree growth occurs in the warmth and light of spring and summer, but growth may also be halted during periods of drought or extreme heat.

How deciduous trees survive

In fall, deciduous trees shed their delicate leaves (see p.42) and enter into a period of dormancy. In dormancy, immature leaves (and sometimes flowers) are held in a protective bud until temperatures increase and they can continue growing without risk of frost damage. Late frosts can affect spring blossom, however, particularly on early-flowering fruit trees.

How evergreen trees keep their leaves

Evergreen trees have evolved to produce glossy or needlelike leaves, which are much more resilient to winter temperatures than the soft leaves of deciduous trees. Evergreens continue to photosynthesize during winter but at a much slower rate.

What's more, some evergreens produce a sort of "antifreeze" to help the tree through winter. When water freezes, it expands and takes up more space, so it can burst the cells of fragile leaves. The evergreens' "antifreeze" comprises a series of hormones and proteins, which keep cell walls intact.

Shrubs

You may see a tree described as a shrub or small tree, which means that it can be grown as either. Hawthorn and elder fall into this category. Generally speaking, shrubs are multistemmed, woody plants with a rounded shape, whereas trees are taller and have a single stem. However, the definitions aren't that simple, as you can have multi-stemmed trees, such as magnolias, and small trees that can also be grown as shrubs or as hedging plants, such as hawthorn and elder.

How you grow or prune the plant can determine whether it develops into a tree or shrub. In my garden, I grow a standard hawthorn tree, but I also have a hawthorn that I'm growing as a hedging plant and another that I'm growing as a shrub.

Trees grow outward and upward, but only from their tips and outer edges.

Your tree through the year

Thinking about how your tree will look from spring to winter may help you decide which to choose. In addition to size and shape and how it fits into your garden and among other plants (see pp.154–155), think about how it will look in different seasons. It's worth considering not only flowers and fruits, but also bark in fall and winter, plus spring catkins and fall leaf color.

Deciduous trees are bare in winter and may be smothered in blossom in spring and fruit in summer, and their leaves may turn shades of red, yellow, orange, and even purple before falling in fall. Evergreen trees retain their leaves, so are less varied through the year, but they may bear flowers and fruits over the seasons.

Spring

Spring comes with rising temperatures and sap, as trees (and the rest of the garden) burst into growth. Leaves unfurl and flowers open, offering potentially dazzling displays of blossom and/or new leaves, which can be a different color to mature leaves. Many trees are renowned for their spring blossom (see pp.38–39)—fruit trees such as apple, pear, and cherry are particularly beautiful, with some having ornamental varieties with even greater amounts of blossom. As well as these fruiting trees, others that boast incredible spring flowers include blackthorn, hawthorn, juneberry, and elderflower. Willows are also worth a mention, as some varieties (such as the Kilmarnock willow) bear spectacular spring catkins that are loved by bees.

Summer

Trees are full of leaf in summer, and some have immature fruits developing. As with winter, summer is normally not a season of spectacular displays, although it's important to take time to appreciate the tree in all its leafy glory and to get outside to listen to the rustle of those wonderful leaves before they fall. It's also vital to consider the tree as a backdrop to other plants. A solid green can be the perfect foil for other colors, so you might plant a flowering shrub, such as weigela, in front of it. Some trees, such as crape myrtle and varieties of dogwood, flower in summer, so if you're after a dazzling summer display, there is some choice available.

Fall

A time of glorious leaf color, fall is when deciduous trees start to enter dormancy (see pp.42–43). Fruiting trees are at their fruitiest in fall, too, and some species, such as crab apples, boast fall leaf color and fruits at the same time. For the best trees for fall color, look no further than Japanese maples, stag's horn sumach, beech, sweet gum, Chinese tupelo, and maidenhair tree (see also pp.124–135).

Winter

In winter, deciduous trees have bare stems, with small leaf and/or flower buds ready to burst into growth in spring. While the skeletal frame of a deciduous tree in winter is a thing of beauty in its own right, in a small space, you might consider one with striking bark, such as Tibetan cherry, paperbark maple, and Himalayan birch. These can form the perfect winter focal point if grown in a prominent position in the garden.

In a small space, you may also plump for an evergreen tree. Evergreen trees largely look the same throughout the year, but some will retain fruit or berries during the winter, adding to their appeal (and their wildlife value). The strawberry tree is a particular highlight, bearing flowers and fruit in winter while retaining its glossy evergreen leaves.

The skeletal frame of a deciduous tree in winter is a thing of beauty.

Spring blossom

One of the most fantastic displays the natural world has to offer is spring blossom. After months of winter, along comes spring with its masses of blousy pink and white flowers. Stand beneath a fruit tree in full blossom and you will hear nothing but the buzz of bees as they zoom from one pollen-loaded flower to another. Spring blossom is life-giving, life-affirming stuff.

While lots of trees flower in spring, "blossom" typically refers to the flowers of trees in the Rosaceae family, which includes apples, cherries, peaches, and pears.

Celebrating blossom

Cherry blossom is particularly celebrated—it's the national flower of Japan, and thousands of people gather together each spring for *hanami*, or to "view the cherry trees." There are hundreds of varieties of ornamental and fruiting cherries. Most ornamentals are cultivars of the Japanese cherry *Prunus cerasus* (or "sakura"). While beautiful, many have double flowers, meaning bees and other pollinators have difficulty accessing the pollen and nectar.

Although cherry blossom is undoubtedly lovely, it's apple blossom that I love the most. In a good year, apple and crab apple trees are so covered in blossom, you can barely see the stems. Most varieties have pink buds that open to pink-blushed white flowers. From a distance, they look like fluffy cumulus clouds, and close up, they roar with the buzz of hundreds of queen bumblebees. To plant a blossom tree in your garden is to plant a firm seasonal marker. You'll spend winter looking for signs of bud burst and spring marveling at its flowers.

Despite not officially being blossom trees, other flowering trees should not be overlooked. The juneberry bears beautiful spring flowers, as does the eastern redbud. Magnolias are also renowned for their variety of gorgeous spring flowers. Just don't call them blossom!

Spring blossom

Fruit, nuts, seeds, and berries

Adding color, interest, and wildlife value, fruit, nuts, seeds, and berries enhance a tree's garden appeal. While many gardeners prefer a fruiting or berrying tree, don't underestimate the beauty of a seeding tree like birch or alder. I love to watch blue tits hanging upside down to eat from my silver birch tree—the seeds might not be that colorful, but the birds are!

Trees, like all plants, reproduce by fertilization, a process that enables them to produce seed for the next generation. Fertilization occurs after pollination, when male pollen comes into contact with female ovaries. Tree flowers are pollinated by insects or wind—fertilized flowers develop into fruit, which takes several forms, including berries, nuts, and cones.

Insect pollination

Many trees, such as apples, cherries, and hawthorn, produce sweet, sugary nectar to attract pollinating insects. Pollinators have different mouthparts. The proboscis (tongue) length varies between bees, butterflies, and moths, while flies have a different type of proboscis altogether. Flowers of all kinds have evolved various shapes to accommodate different mouths. Insect-pollinated trees can have male and female flowers on the same tree or on separate trees. Some flowers contain male and female parts within the same bloom; these are known as hermaphrodites. This doesn't always mean they are self-fertile, however. You may be familiar with the need for a "pollination partner" for apple trees (see p.151). This is because, despite having hermaphrodite flowers, many apple trees still need to be cross-pollinated with another tree.

When insects visit flowers, they either collect pollen intentionally, or it "accidentally" attaches to their body as they are feeding on nectar. The more flowers they visit, the more pollen is transferred on and off their bodies. Some bees are particularly good at pollination: honeybees and bumblebees comb pollen off their bodies into neat "baskets" on their hind legs, but others carry pollen in a rough "brush" on their abdomen. This increases the chance of pollen falling from their body as they visit new flowers, resulting in fertilization.

Wind pollination

Some trees, including oaks, release pollen into the air in the hope that wind will carry it to the ovaries. Conifers are also wind-pollinated, but they bear male and female cones instead of flowers.

How fruits, nuts, seeds, and berries form

After fertilization, the female flower parts develop into a fruit containing seeds. The fruit can be fleshy like a berry, apple, or cherry or can be papery and winged like a samara (on sycamores, birches, and elms). As trees can't move, they have evolved ways for their seeds to travel to a variety of places. Fruits and berries can be eaten by a mammal or bird and the seed dispersed to grow elsewhere, potentially miles from the original tree. Samaras can be lifted and carried on the wind. Some fruits, such as coconuts, float on water and can start a new generation on a different land mass.

Many "nuts," including almonds and walnuts, are actually fruits known as drupes—the part we eat is the seed, which is within a fleshy layer. True nuts, such as hazelnuts, acorns, and chestnuts, are botanically described as dry, single-seeded fruits. They are formed when the ovary wall of a fertilized flower hardens into a tough shell. The same fertilization process results in so many different outcomes. Isn't nature amazing?

Flowers have evolved various shapes to accommodate different mouths of pollinators.

Fall leaf color

Planting a tree for fall color is planting light in darkness. Just as the flowers fade and the garden starts to recede, along comes the tree with a whole new color palette. I love my silver birch most in fall, when its heart-shaped leaves turn a glorious buttery yellow. It's the first thing I see when I look out of the window, and when the sun catches its leaves, my heart melts a little.

Besides the silver birch, my hawthorn and mountain ash provide color with fat, red berries, and the hawthorn sometimes displays red leaves, too. But many deciduous trees look good in fall, with oranges, reds, and yellows dominating as a final flourish before winter sets in.

The orange and yellow pigments in leaves are actually present all year round, but we can't see them because they're hidden by the dominant green pigment, chlorophyll, which is needed for photosynthesis to make glucose (food for the tree). Some leaves also contain red-pink pigments (anthocyanins), which are equally hidden by the chlorophyll.

Toward the end of summer, the tree stops producing chlorophyll and no longer relies on photosynthesis as a source of energy, using stored glucose instead. As the leaves die back, the green pigments break down first to reveal the other hidden pigments. The intensity and stability of the red-pink pigments differ according to how much glucose a tree has stored, soil acidity, temperature, and other factors. This means that fall color can vary widely from year to year.

At this point, the leaves are no longer working to produce food for the tree. The vessels that connect the leaf to the tree are closed off and a layer of cells between the leaf stalk and the twig holding it, known as the abscission layer, increases in size. This process severs the leaf from its twig without leaving a wound. The tree enters dormancy, saving its energy over winter for its next big moment: spring.

The tree's role in your garden

The tree in your garden will have three key roles: one for you and those who live with you, including your neighbors; one for the other trees, plants, and fungi growing around it; and one for the wildlife—from the tiniest insects, such as aphids and leafminers, to the birds that land in its branches and the small mammals that rest in its holes and hibernate beneath its fallen leaves.

People root themselves to their garden tree. They mark the seasons by its different looks: spring by masses of blossom, fall by leaf color and/or fruit, and winter by a skeleton frame or vivid bark or (if it's evergreen) glossy leaves and berries.

The tree and you
Noticing changes in a tree over the seasons is mindful. This mindfulness helps distract us from other things that may be dragging us down and helps improve our mental health. Watching each season unfold reminds us that the world is still turning—that these ancient natural processes of bud burst and flowering and fruiting and leaf fall are still intact.

You might sit beneath your tree and listen to its leaves rustling or its sap rising. You might watch birds perch on its branches or squirrels scamper up and down its trunk. When its leaves shed in fall, you might spot blackbirds turning them over in search of grubs. You might stand, transfixed, as a robin stuffs berries into its mouth.

Planting a tree is the ultimate in self-care because, from the moment you plant it, you will never stop being in love with its processes, its stature, and its function in the garden. To plant a tree is to invest in the future, yes, but to plant a tree is also to invest in yourself. Because trees are inherently good for you.

And it's not just you who will benefit from it—your neighbors, too, some of whom you will never have met, may love your tree. They too will track its seasons—its fall color and spring blossom. They too will

44

enjoy the birds your tree brings, for they won't land in your garden alone, but in other gardens, too. Don't forget that, by planting your tree, you're providing a service for your community (see pp.50–51)—just as people will stop to admire a pretty front garden, so they will enjoy a tree, even from a couple of streets away.

More practically, your tree will provide shade from the hottest sun, add height and structure to your garden, and create a focal point. You might plant it in front of an unsightly building you want to hide or in a position that blocks your view of a neighbor's window, giving you more privacy. More practical still, it will hold water in the earth with its roots, doing its small part to avert flooding. If you plant your tree in an urban area, it will contribute to the cooling of city temperatures (see pp.26–28). The leaves of your tree will also buffer wind and absorb polluting particles, something we will benefit from now and in years to come.

The tree and your garden

Trees connect with other trees, shrubs, and plants via their root systems and the fungal threads (hyphae) that grow around them (see p.22). Trees do better when planted in small groups, as they feed and communicate with each other via their root systems, aided by fungi. If you have room to plant more than one tree, then please do. If not, perhaps your neighbor has a tree that yours can connect with?

The tree and wildlife

The best trees for wildlife provide a range of different food types and habitats for a wide variety of species, including insects and their larvae and birds.

Native trees tend to be better for wildlife than non-natives (see pp.20–21). Moths and other flying insects can lay eggs on the leaves, and birds will take the resulting larvae and feed them to their chicks in the nest. As your tree grows, it might develop fissures in its bark, which can shelter hibernating insects. As it ages, holes will appear in the trunk, which will provide nesting sites for birds and small mammals. Gaps between the roots might fill with water and provide the perfect habitat for hoverflies to lay their eggs, while a dry hole might be large enough for a groundhog. A tree is an ecosystem in its own right, a city that hundreds of species might call home.

Finding the right spot

Before you reach for the spade to plant your tree, you'll need to think about the impact it will have on you and your neighbors. Pay attention to where the light falls in the garden and how much shade will be cast in yours and your neighbors' spaces. Don't just think about the tree—and the garden—now, but also how they will change over the next 20 years or more.

It's a sad fact that trees and hedges are a frequent cause of neighborly disputes. Common complaints arise from hedges and trees growing too tall and casting too much shade, while those that drop a lot of leaves or seeds can be problematic, too. The last thing you want is to fall out with your neighbors, so plan carefully. It may be worth chatting with them beforehand. They might offer some advice or even be inspired to plant a tree of their own!

Think about shade

Depending on where the sun hits your garden, planting your tree on one side or end of the space means it could cast less shade on neighboring plots. If you think shade is likely to be an issue, avoid trees with large, dense canopies (such as evergreens). Trees with an airy canopy, such as silver birch and some types of palm, cast only dappled shade rather than deep shade, so they can be a happy compromise in a built-up area.

It's also worth thinking about how much shade is already cast in your garden. Most trees eventually grow to a height where their leaves can access the sun (it's how they evolved to be trees in the first place), so planting a tree on the north-facing side of your garden won't be a problem in the long term—if a fence casts shade, your tree will easily grow beyond it. However, buildings and other trees cast shade that could block much-needed light from your tree. Some trees are more tolerant of shade than others—typically, flowering and fruiting trees need a lot of sun to help ripen their fruits, but foliage trees can cope with less light. Bear in mind, however, that the best fall colors result from trees that have had a lot of summer sun (see p.42).

Planting near buildings

Trees near buildings don't usually cause damage, but some can. Tree roots can affect drains and paving, or in rare cases cause subsidence, while branches can affect roofs and guttering. Subsidence is more likely with houses built before the 1950s, as they have shallower foundations than those built today. This is most likely if you have clay soil, which can shrink in prolonged periods of drought. Older houses also have older drainage systems, making it more likely that tree roots can enter and block them.

In the US, there are few rules on the distance a tree should be planted from a house. How far you plant your tree from your house should depend on how old the house is and the type of tree you choose. A fruit tree grafted onto a dwarfing rootstock will not have the root run of a mighty oak and will never grow as tall as your roof and guttering. But large deciduous trees—particularly those with suckering roots, such as elm— should be avoided.

As a general rule, trees extend their roots out to the equivalent distance of between half and the whole tree's height. More drought-tolerant trees have less reliance on water and so have smaller root systems. Look at the eventual height of your tree, its drought tolerance, your soil type, and the age of your house and do what's best for you. I planted my trees 40ft (12m) from my Victorian house, but the mountain ash is only 16ft (5m) from my neighbors' new-build. Its canopy could grow to up to 26ft (8m) after 50 years (13ft/4m on either side of the trunk), and some branches may need to be pruned annually to protect guttering. On my loamy soil, the roots won't be an issue.

Integrating the tree into your garden

It's also important to consider how your tree will affect the look of your garden. Over time, it will become a huge presence, adding height and structure, becoming a focal point that will draw your eye across the garden. Use this to your advantage—create an attractive border around the tree (see pp.154–155), adding shrubs and herbaceous plants that will not only look good, but will grow in harmony with your tree, as well as providing additional habitats for birds, bees, and other wildlife.

Choose a tree that fits the scale of your garden: a full-sized tree isn't always the best option. The space may be too small or shady, or your neighbors may have already shown concern at the potential shade cast on their garden. Luckily, there are some alternatives to consider.

Hedging

A hedge is a wonderful thing, made simply by planting trees very close together (at 12in/30cm intervals) and cutting them back every one to two years. In small spaces, you can maintain a height of just 3ft (1m) and plant in single rows so the hedge doesn't grow too wide. Or, if you have more room, plant in double rows for a thicker hedge and let it grow to a height of 6½ft (2m) or more.

Hedges are great for small urban spaces, not only because they can be trimmed to size, but because they can absorb more polluting particles than trees, as they grow closer to the ground (the perfect height to absorb particles from cars). They still absorb carbon dioxide and drink water, and they have wildlife value, too. Hedges provide a natural boundary to gardens and enable wildlife to travel more

easily between them while also offering shelter for anything from nesting birds to hibernating hedgehogs. What's more, hedges filter the wind, helping slow it down. Such a wind break can be a godsend in exposed gardens and could provide a great solution to windier conditions caused by climate change.

Some trees lend themselves better to hedging than others—evergreen trees such as yew make particularly dense hedges, while regular trimming keeps beech trees in their juvenile state so their fall leaves remain on throughout winter, to beautiful effect. A mixed native hedge of hawthorn, hazel, blackthorn, and field rose makes a wonderful wildlife habitat, providing food and homes for a huge range of species.

Espalier and fan-trained trees

Fan-trained and espalier trees are usually fruit trees grown against a wall or fence, trained as either a fan shape or as a series of "tiers" known as an espalier. They are a fantastic way to grow fruit in a small space, and they are gloriously ornamental. You can even grow fan- and espalier-trained trees on wires between posts. I have such an "espalier boundary" between mine and my neighbors' allotment plots. Between us, we have two apple and three pear trees, and we share the fruit each year.

Apples and pears can be trained in a number of ways, including as fans and espaliers. Cherries, peaches, plums, and apricots are fan-trained only (see p.151). All are sold either as whips (young trees) that you train yourself or as pretrained trees you can plant and then prune annually. They're all easy to grow and produce a surprising amount of fruit.

Growing trees in pots

If you have a really small space, live in rented housing, or have very poor soil, you could grow a tree in a pot. Only very small trees are suitable, but some have been developed for this purpose. Apples grown on dwarfing rootstocks do well in pots, while slow-growing Japanese maples and flowering dogwoods make fantastic ornamental choices. For a formal, evergreen display, choose olive, yew, or bay. Or for a sunny, sheltered site, you might go for a lemon or fig. A tree's root run in a pot will never match that of free ground, so you will need to water and feed it regularly to ensure it grows well. Mulching or replacing the top few centimeters of soil annually will keep soil fresh.

Climbers

In even smaller spaces, if you can't fit in another tree and hedges aren't an option, look to climbers. Most are easy to grow and can be as tall and dense as trees and hedges. Ivy has incredible value, absorbing pollutants and providing homes for wildlife. Honeysuckle and clematis, climbing and rambling roses, and jasmine are other possibilities.

A mixed native hedge of hawthorn, hazel, blackthorn, and field rose makes a wonderful wildlife habitat.

The tree in the community

In urban and now more suburban areas in the US, there are homes that have little to no garden space. If you don't have a garden, how do you plant a tree? In your community, of course! You can join a community group, set one up, or get involved in planting trees in a local park or green space.

There are thousands of community groups across the country. Some use pockets of land for communal gardens and nature reserves, while others help maintain parks. I've seen allotments on old railway tracks, "secret gardens" in church grounds, and planting groups on corners of pavement. Even planters on your city street can be used to green your area.

Joining a community group

If you want to get involved with your community, find out what groups already exist. Look for "Friends of" groups, covering all sorts from parks to nature reserves, small community gardens, allotments, and squares. Check your local area's Facebook page, search gardening association sites, or visit your park or green space to see if there are posters advertising such a group. You can even set up your own.

Planting in a communal space

There are other options apart from a group. Contact your local arboreal (tree) team. You may be able to "donate" a tree to a local park, which the arboreal team plants and maintains for a fee. Planting in green spaces such as parks and community gardens is much easier and cheaper than street trees (see pp.28–29), but consult your local government first. They will let you know if there are cables underground or access is needed, and they'll also need to know, as it's likely that they will maintain them. Never plant trees without permission— you could be creating a headache for someone later on.

TREE PROFILES

If you plant only one tree, make sure it's the right one for you and your garden. Discover 50 garden trees, with options for spring blossom and other flowers, berries, fruits and seeds, plus evergreens and palms. You'll also find ideas for large and small outdoor spaces, along with tips for helping wildlife and growing trees in a changing climate.

SMALL
TREES

For those of us with smaller gardens and outdoor spaces, as well as urban gardens where plot size, shade, and neighbors are considerations, small trees are an obvious choice. Many can be grown in containers on patios, roof gardens, and balconies. Small trees come in a variety of shapes and sizes and can be evergreen or deciduous, flowering and/or fruiting, good for wildlife and highly ornamental. While a few trees in this selection can grow as tall as 39ft (12m) (most are much smaller), they are slow-growing and may take many years to reach this size. You'll find small trees in other categories, too, such as Fruit trees (see pp.64–77) and Trees for fall color (see pp.124–135).

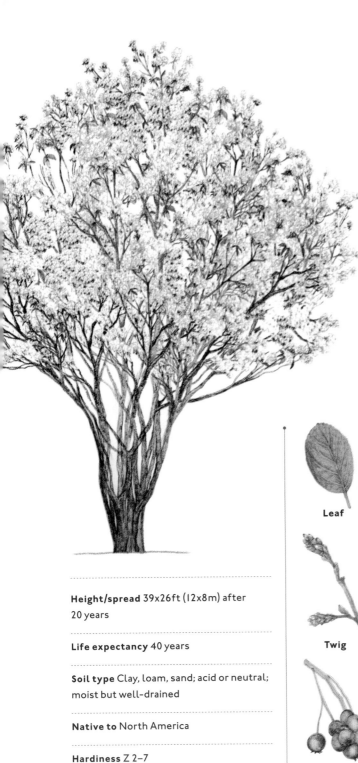

SERVICEBERRY

Amelanchier lamarckii

An attractively shaped, often multistemmed, tree, serviceberry has coppery pink young leaves bursting just as masses of snow-white, star-shaped flowers appear in spring.

Serviceberry works well as a feature in a lawn or as part of a mixed ornamental border or hedge. The leaves mature to a yellow-green before turning vivid shades of red in fall. The red-purple berries are used to decorate desserts such as muffins, pies, and cheesecakes in North America. They are also popular with garden birds.

There are several hybrid cultivars of serviceberry, such as *Amelanchier × grandiflora* 'Ballerina', which has a more upright habit than *A. lamarckii*, and *A. × grandiflora* 'Robin Hill', which has beautiful pink flowers.

Leaf

Twig

Berries

ID NOTES

Leaves Oblong, papery, tinted bronze in spring; red in fall

Twigs Reddish, with occasional gray mottling

Flowers Star-shaped, white

Fruit Dark red-purple edible berries

Bark Smooth and gray with faint lines and gray spots developing with age

CARE NOTES

Grow in full sun for the best flowering, fruiting, and fall color. If growing as a hedge, plant 6½ft (2m) apart. Serviceberry doesn't need regular pruning, but it pays to remove dead or crossing stems after flowering. Mulch in fall with homemade compost or well-rotted manure.

Height/spread 39x26ft (12x8m) after 20 years

Life expectancy 40 years

Soil type Clay, loam, sand; acid or neutral; moist but well-drained

Native to North America

Hardiness Z 2–7

ID NOTES

Leaves Up to 2½in (6cm) long, glossy, and oval with rounded teeth; in fall, usually yellow but sometimes red, orange, and purple

Twigs Grayish, developing cracks with age, bearing pointed leaf buds with fine, downy hairs on short stalks; twigs may sometimes develop spines in exposed areas

Flowers Five petals and may be white, pink, or red

Fruit/seed Small, applelike fruits, usually red or yellow

Bark Gray-brown, flecked

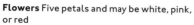

Leaf

Twig

Flower

Fruit

Malus sylvestris

TREE PROFILES

CRAB APPLE

Malus spp.

Perfect for small gardens, crab apples are compact and look good almost all year. In spring, they bear masses of blossom, which develops into colorful fall fruits that last well into winter. Some species have dramatic fall foliage, too. Crab apples are excellent for wildlife, with flowers and fruit used by a variety of species. They're also handy for gardeners—they're often grown as a "pollination partner" (see p.151) for edible apples to help them produce more fruit.

Most crab apples can be grown as a large shrub or small tree, with some species bearing double flowers or unusual leaf coloring. They really are gorgeous trees.

Crab apple blossom is invaluable to pollinators—particularly bees—and the fruit of many varieties is used to make crab apple jelly. Any fruit left on the tree provides food for birds and small mammals in winter. Crab apples can also host mistletoe, a semiparasitic plant that grows in the bark of some species. The well-known crab apple species *Malus sylvestris* is usually grown as a tree but is also used in hedging.

There are around 40 other crab apple species native to Europe, Asia, and North America, including *M. sargentii* and *M. floribunda*, which are both multistemmed. Most trees available to buy are derived from one or more of these species.

CARE NOTES

Only light pruning is usually necessary for trees, with the removal of dead and crossing stems a priority (see p.159). Some species benefit from the lowest stems being removed to "lift" the canopy. Crab apples are susceptible to a number of pests and diseases, including apple scab, fireblight, codling moth, and cedar-apple rust. Usually, the tree can live quite happily while affected and there's no need to take any action. Pests such as aphids are part of the natural ecosystem and will be eaten by predators such as birds and wasps.

Height/spread 16x13ft (5x4m) after 20 years

Life expectancy 70 years

Soil type Clay, loam, sand; acid, alkaline, or neutral; moist but well-drained

Native to Europe, North America, Asia

Hardiness Z 3–8

BRONZE LOQUAT

Eriobotrya deflexa

Highly ornamental if you're after a tropical look, bronze loquat has evergreen growth that gives it year-round appeal in small spaces.

It has a neat, compact habit, making it ideal for growing in pots or training as a standard or even as an espalier tree (see p.151). Its dense canopy means it can also make a good screen. The leathery leaves can grow to 12in (30cm) and have almost white undersides. As well as having striking leaves, bronze loquat produces small flowers and may bear medlarlike fruit. Farther north, summers may not be warm enough for the fruit to ripen enough to be edible, unless it is unusually hot. However, with climate change, growing your own loquat fruit could be in the cards in future.

ID NOTES

Leaves Evergreen glossy, oblong, and green, up to 8in (20cm) long; felted undersides

Twigs Green and thick

Flowers Small and pink-white, borne in panicles with a hawthornlike scent

Fruit/seed Fuzzy, edible fruit like a cross between apples and apricots, with a sharp taste

Bark Thin and easily damaged

CARE NOTES

Hardy to 14°F (-10°C), bronze loquat may suffer damage in winter. Have some horticultural fleece handy to protect the leaves if temperatures dip below 14°F (-10°C), or, if growing in a pot, move indoors until temperatures increase again.

Leaf

Flower

Fruit

Height/spread 26x26ft (8x8m) after 20 years

Life expectancy 30–50 years

Soil type Chalk, clay, loam, sand; acid, alkaline, or neutral; moist but well-drained

Native to China and Japan

Hardiness Z 9–12

SOFT TREE FERN

Dicksonia antarctica

Tree ferns are not strictly trees,
but with their trunklike stems and
crown of fronds, they look like them
and play the same role in the garden.

A tree fern's "trunk" is actually its root
system and is covered in masses of aerial
roots, which take much of the tree's water
and nutrients from the humid atmosphere.
This means, in dry conditions, you may
have to water the trunk to keep it moist.

Tree ferns are extremely slow-growing—
1in (2.5cm) per year—so buy as mature a
specimen as you can afford. They work well
in urban spaces, including courtyards, and
as part of a woodland planting scheme (with
an exotic twist!). Despite being native to
Tasmania, which rarely has temperatures
below freezing, tree ferns are hardy to 16°F
(-9°C) for short periods, although they will
lose their leaves, and it's important to ensure
the trunk doesn't freeze. For the best chance
of survival, grow them in a humid, shady spot.

Height/spread 8x6½ft (2.5x2m) after
20–50 years

Life expectancy 500 years

Soil type Clay, loam; neutral or acid;
boggy, moist

Native to Tasmania

Hardiness Z 9–11

Trunk

Frond

ID NOTES

Leaves Fernlike fronds

Fruit/seed Doesn't produce seeds but has tiny
spores on the undersides of the fronds

Bark Matted, fibrous network of roots

CARE NOTES

In winter, protect the trunk and growing
point at the top by wrapping them in the
old fronds, along with some straw and
horticultural fleece. This will stop the
tree's root system from freezing or drying
out and should ensure new fronds sprout
from the top of the tree in spring.

OLIVE

Olea europaea

One of the oldest known cultivated trees, the olive was traditionally grown for its fruit, as well as being a symbol of happiness and peace. The average lifespan of olive trees is 300–600 years, with the oldest recorded at 2,000 years old. Olives make popular evergreen garden trees in parts of the Sunbelt, bearing silvery gray, oval leaves; inconspicuous white flowers; and, occasionally, edible olives.

Olives are highly ornamental and easy to grow. They do best—and are more likely to produce fruit—in sun, and they tolerate poor soils. Slow-growing, they do well in pots. You can train an olive as a standard—with a long single stem; a pair of standards looks good on either side of a doorway. In colder areas, they may need winter protection.

Olives are wind pollinated. If you're lucky, your olive tree may start producing fruit after three to five years. You can harvest the olives when they're green, but it's best if you can wait until they're black and starting to fall from the branches.

Freshly harvested olives are bitter to taste. To make them palatable, simply soak the olives in water for 10 days, changing the water every day. Store them in jars of brine (salted water) for about four weeks before eating.

CARE NOTES

Very little pruning is needed. However, in late spring or early summer, remove dead, diseased, or dying branches (see pp.158–159). For standard trees, treat your olive as any other fruit tree, thinning out branches to create an open, bowl-shaped center, where light and air can reach developing fruit. Avoid pruning too hard, as this will result in nonfruiting "water shoots," which are weaker and more susceptible to disease than regular branches.

For winter protection of olives in pots, if needed, you can buy a fleece jacket that you pop over the crown of the tree like a bag, then tighten around the stem with a drawstring.

Height/spread 26x10ft (8 x 3m) after 20 years

Life expectancy 300 years

Soil type Clay, loam, sand; acid, alkaline, or neutral; moist but well-drained

Native to Europe

Hardiness Z 8–10

ID NOTES

Leaves Leathery, silvery gray-green, oval, and narrow, up to 3in (7.5cm) long

Twigs Smooth and gray

Flowers Tiny and white, borne in racemes up to 2in (5cm) long

Fruit Green drupes (olives), ripening to black, with a central stone

Bark Smooth and gray when young, aging to rugged and gnarled

Fruit

Bark

Flower

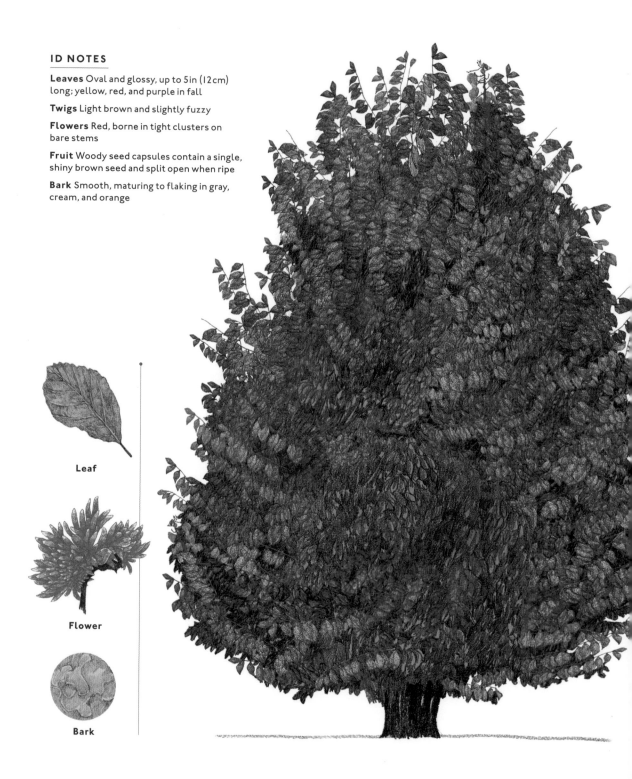

ID NOTES

Leaves Oval and glossy, up to 5in (12cm) long; yellow, red, and purple in fall

Twigs Light brown and slightly fuzzy

Flowers Red, borne in tight clusters on bare stems

Fruit Woody seed capsules contain a single, shiny brown seed and split open when ripe

Bark Smooth, maturing to flaking in gray, cream, and orange

Leaf

Flower

Bark

62

PERSIAN IRONWOOD

Parrotia persica

Famed for its fall color, the glossy, ribbed, midgreen leaves
of Persian ironwood turn incredible shades of yellow, orange,
red, and purple in fall. What's more, the tree holds onto
its leaves for longer than many other species, so its
display can last for several weeks.

Following leaf fall, it's only another few weeks before Persian ironwood lights up again in late winter to spring, with tight clusters of red flowers that form dramatically on bare branches. The bark is attractive as well—silvery gray in color, it starts to flake away as it matures, revealing young bark underneath in beautiful shades of pink, green, and yellow.

Persian ironwood is native to Iran and the Caucasus and is a member of the Hamamelidae (witch hazel) family. Its flowers bear similarities to witch hazel flowers. The cultivar 'Vanessa' is a more upright version than the species, making it more suitable for gardens. It will thrive in all soils, but its fall color is best in slightly acidic soil.

CARE NOTES

Very little pruning is needed. Simply remove
crossing and dead branches in late winter to
early spring. Any reshaping or reducing of size
should be done at this time, too.

Height/spread 26x26ft (8x8m) after 20 years

Life expectancy 150 years

Soil type Chalk, clay, loam, sand; acid,
alkaline, or neutral; moist but well-drained

Native to Northern Iran to the Caucasus

Hardiness Z 5–8

FRUIT
TREES

A fruit tree not only provides interest and wildlife value, but
blossom and edible fruit, too. A mature apple or pear tree,
for example, provides food and habitats for a huge range of
species, as well as fruit for you to eat fresh and use in
cooking. Fruit tree blossom is hugely important to early
pollinators in spring. Many species can be trained as espalier
or fan trees against a fence or wall (see p.151), helping the
fruit ripen and making them excellent for small gardens.
Leave windfalls for wildlife and don't worry about "pests"
attacking the fruit. We all have to eat—simply cut around
any tunnels or other signs of damage and look at ways you
can increase predator numbers in your garden if the pests
seem to be getting the upper hand.

Leaf

Twig

Flower

Height/spread 13x13ft (4x4m) after 20 years

Life expectancy 50 years

Soil type Clay, loam, sand; neutral; moist but well-drained

Native to Europe

Hardiness Z 5–7

PLUM

- -

Prunus domestica

With their attractive blossom, fruit, and wildlife value, plum trees make fantastic small garden trees.

Plums, gages, and damsons are closely related. Plums are large and usually soft. Gages are smaller, round, and sweet, while Mirabelle plums are smaller still and range from yellow to dark pink. Damsons have a spicy, tart flavor and are used in cooking, particularly in jam. When buying, check the cultivar's pollination needs. Many are self-fertile, but others need another plum nearby to aid fertilization. All can be fan-trained to save space (using a dwarfing rootstock, see pp.150–151). 'Victoria' is an all-round plum, self-fertile, and crops well; 'Avalon' has large, red plums. Plum leaves are a foodplant for several moth species; the flowers are used by bees; and the fruit is eaten by birds, insects, and small mammals.

ID NOTES

Leaves Dark green, oval with small teeth and sometimes downy undersides

Twigs Dark brown, straight, sometimes spiny

Flowers White, with five petals, borne in clusters at the same time as the leaves form

Fruit/seed Large, fleshy fruit (drupe) with one large seed or stone

Bark Dark brown

CARE NOTES

Prune in summer to avoid silver leaf disease (see p.167), making an open bowl shape (see p.161). Mulch in fall to suppress weeds and retain moisture.

APPLE

Malus domestica

Apple trees come in all shapes and sizes and make popular garden trees, as
they're easy to grow and provide years of ornamental value and enjoyment.
The species *Malus domestica* is thought to have derived from the wild species
M. sieversii. Apples have been cultivated for thousands of years, and there are
around 7,500 cultivated varieties.

Traditionally, apples grew to some 100ft
(30m) tall, but now most are grafted onto
rootstocks, which control their size and shape
(see pp.150–151). Apples can be grown as
standards (standalone trees with a single stem)
or trained as espaliers against a wall, fence, or
wires (see p.151). There are more innovative
types, such as cordons, which can be trained
as a low hedge, and "family" apple trees, with
several varieties grafted onto one rootstock.

For the best fruit crop, most apples need a
"pollination partner." This is a different type
of apple (or crab apple, pp.56–57) that flowers
at the same time and helps pollination. The
enormous variety of cultivars ranges from
commonly grown 'Cox's Orange Pippin'
and 'Spartan' to lesser-known 'Ashmead's
Kernel' and 'Claygate Pearmain'. Many
old apple varieties are linked to specific
geographical regions.

Apples are hugely beneficial to wildlife.
Their flowers provide food for pollinators
in spring, particularly types of mason bee.
Their bark and leaves are used by various
invertebrates, while windfalls are eaten
by birds, butterflies, and small mammals.

CARE NOTES

Make sure you choose the right rootstock
for your purpose. Espaliers usually grow
on MM106 rootstock, while standards are
grown on M25.

Apples need regular pruning, particularly
if you're growing them as espaliers. Prune
standards in winter, removing crossing and
dead branches and helping create an open,
bowl shape (see pp.160–161). Prune espaliers
in both summer and winter, cutting back
sideshoots to maintain the espalier shape
(see p.161).

Height/spread Up to 26x26ft (8x8m) after
20 years, depending on rootstock

Life expectancy 50–100 years

Soil type Clay, loam, sand; neutral; moist
but well-drained

Native to Central Asia

Hardiness Z 3–8

TREE PROFILES

ID NOTES

Leaves Dark green, oval with serrated margins, variable length up to 3in (7cm)

Twigs Red/brown with short shoots and fuzzy leaf buds

Flowers Inflorescences of up to six, each with five petals, appearing in spring at the same time as the leaves unfurl

Fruit Edible apple with five chambers, each containing a number of seeds known as "pips"

Bark Red/gray speckled with white spots (lenticels), maturing to gray/brown and flaky

Leaf

Fruit

Flower

ID NOTES

Leaves Dark green, oval with pointed tips and long stalks; yellow in fall

Twigs Spiny, gray

Flowers White, with five petals, borne in clusters

Fruit Edible pears up to 5in (12cm) long

Bark Gray-brown

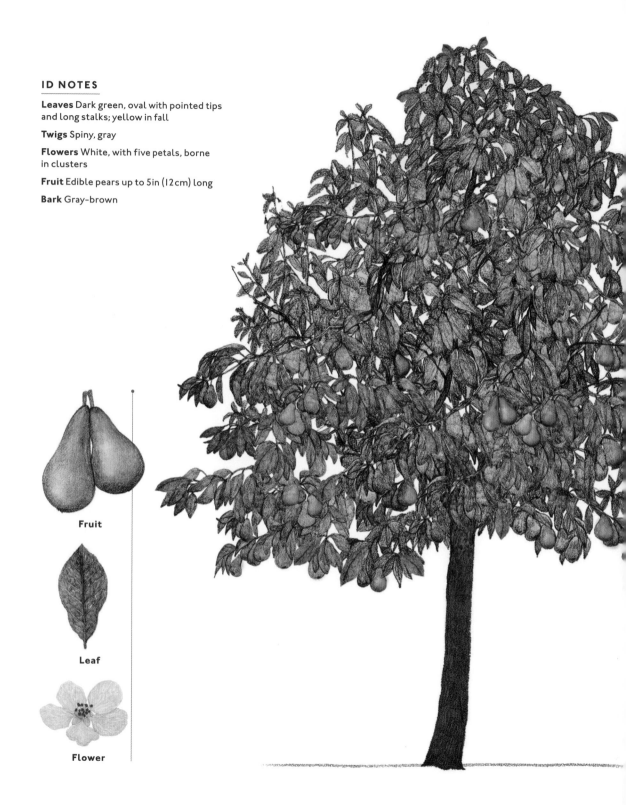

Fruit

Leaf

Flower

PEAR

Pyrus communis

Cultivated in Europe for thousands of years, pears come in many types and in a range of colors, shapes, and sizes, ripening at different times. With their spring blossom and fall fruit, they provide a long season of interest and are attractive to wildlife. There are also some ornamental pears that make excellent garden trees.

Like apples, pears are grown on different rootstocks to manage eventual shape and size (see pp.150–151). Pears are grown on quince rootstocks; Quince A or C are the most appropriate for a garden. They can also be trained as espalier trees against a fence or wall (see p.151). There's a huge variety of pears to choose from, with fruit ranging in color from green to dark red. Like apples, most pears do best with a "pollination partner," which should be a different pear variety that flowers at the same time. If you have space for two pears, then grow two, or check with neighbors to see if there are any growing locally.

Pears are also extremely valuable to wildlife. Bees and other insects use the blossom, while birds, small mammals, and some insects eat the fruit. The leaves are used by moths, and other insects shelter in the bark of mature trees.

Weeping pear (*Pyrus salicifolia* 'Pendula') is a small, ornamental pear with silvery, willowlike foliage and cream-white flowers, then inedible green fruit. It's a useful tree for small gardens and copes well with pollution.

CARE NOTES

Prune pear trees in winter. First, remove crossing and dead branches, and aim for an open habit for standards (see pp.160–161). Prune espalier and fan-trained pears in summer and winter (see p.161). Pears are prone to leaf rust, visible as orange spots on the leaves in summer and eventually cankers on the stems. The fungus relies on junipers to complete its life cycle. Removing leaves can do more harm than good, but pruning out cankers in winter can help keep the problem under control.

Height/spread 39x26ft (12x8m) after 20 years on its own roots; 13x6½ft (4x2m) on a quince rootstock

Life expectancy 50–150 years

Soil type Clay, loam, sand; acid, alkaline, or neutral; moist but well-drained

Native to Temperate regions of Europe, North Africa, and Asia

Hardiness Z 4–9

CHERRY

Prunus spp.

This huge genus encompasses cherries grown mainly for their edible fruit, as well as other more ornamental cherries grown mainly for their blossom (see pp.38–39). Cherries bear blossom in spring, fruit in fall, and have glorious fall color. They're great for wildlife, too—open, single cherry flowers provide food for bees, the fruit is eaten by birds (sorry—but it's good to share!), and the leaves are nibbled by various invertebrate species.

Many fruiting cultivars have been bred from the British native (*Prunus avium*) and bird cherry (*P. padus*). All are grafted onto rootstocks that make them smaller and more manageable. Some cherries can be fan-trained and grown against a wall or fence to save space. Most are sweet to taste, but the sour cherry (*P. cerasus*) bears bitter-tasting cherries on longer stalks. These cherries are excellent in cooked dishes, such as cherry pie.

There's a huge variety of flowering cherries, which make excellent garden trees. Many of these are derived from Japanese species and can be tall, dwarf, columnar, or weeping in habit. *P.* 'Amanogawa' is particularly small, with flowers ranging from white to dark pink. One flowering cherry, *P.* × *subhirtella* 'Autumnalis', flowers in fall. Many have striking bark, making them extra valuable in winter. Bear in mind that, while flowering cherries are very beautiful, only the single-flowered species provide food for pollinators. Cherries on ornamental trees have not been bred for flavor and are unpleasant to eat.

CARE NOTES

Ornamental cherries don't need pruning, unless it's to remove crossing or dead branches (see pp.158–159). Prune edible cherries in summer to avoid silver leaf disease (see p.167), removing crossing and dead branches and shaping the tree to have an open habit. Older trees need little pruning—bear in mind that sweet cherries fruit on wood that's at least a year old, while sour cherries fruit on the previous year's wood, so hard pruning will result in no fruit for at least a year. Cherries are prone to bacterial canker (see p166), visible as leafless branches or branches with small leaves; sunken bark; and distorted, swollen, or cracked patches.

Height/spread Up to 100ft (30m) after 20 years, but will vary due to cultivar and rootstock

Life expectancy 60 years

Soil type Clay, loam, chalk, sand; acid, alkaline, or neutral; moist but well-drained

Native to Europe, Asia, and parts of North Africa

Hardiness Z 4–9

ID NOTES

Leaves Fresh green, oval, pointed and toothed, with pointed tips; yellow, orange, and red in fall

Twigs Variable, bearing clusters of oval-shaped buds

Flowers Pink or white, five-petaled and cup-shaped, borne in clusters; some cultivars have been bred to have more petals

Fruit Round, red cherries with a single seed, or stone, inside

Bark Variable, shiny in some species (such as bird cherry)

Leaf

Fruit

Flower

Prunus avium

Fruit trees

ID NOTES

Leaves 6¼in (16cm) long and 1¼in (3cm) wide, lanceolate (wider in the middle) in shape; golden/red in fall

Twigs New growth is green/red, fading to brown/gray; leaf buds are blunt

Flowers Pink, five-petaled, ¾–1¼in (2–3cm) diameter, appearing on bare stems

Fruit Flesh surrounding a hard seed (drupe). Fuzzy, hair-coated fruits are known as peaches and smooth fruits as nectarines

Bark Dark gray, smooth when young, maturing to scaly

Fruit

Twig

Flower

TREE PROFILES

PEACH

Prunus persica

Providing ornamental value from spring to fall, as well as delicious fruit, peach trees are perfect for small gardens. Growing to no more than 13ft (4m) in height and with an average life expectancy of up to 20 years, they're a good choice if you want to plant something short-term—there's no risk of regretting your planting decisions 50 years later.

Despite being fully hardy, peach trees flower early in the year, which puts the flowers (and the resulting fruits) at risk of frost damage. If you want a reliable source of peaches (or nectarines), you'll need to grow them in a sheltered spot. Outside the warmer portions of the US, peaches may be trained as fans (see p.151) against a south-facing wall to help ensure fruit production. They're also a good option for growing in containers.

The *persica* part of the peach's species name refers to Persia (Iran), where peaches have been cultivated for thousands of years. However, peaches originate in China.

Peach blossom is valuable to pollinators but, as it appears so early, only a few species get to see it. To ensure fertilization, it may be best to hand-pollinate peaches by gently passing a small paintbrush over each flower.

Nectarines are closely related to peaches and have the same growing requirements and nutritional values but lack the fuzzy peach skin. It's said that peaches are more suitable for baking, as the cooking process softens them, while nectarines remain firm.

CARE NOTES

Protect early flowers with two or three layers of horticultural fleece, which you simply drape over the tree to stop frost from reaching the blossom. This needs to be removed during the day. Peaches are prone to the fungal disease peach leaf curl, which distorts leaves and causes them to fall prematurely, resulting in a loss of vigor. As the spores are spread by rain splash, erecting a lean-to rain shelter with plastic sheeting can help stop the spread of the disease. Alternatively, grow your peach tree in a greenhouse or other sheltered environment or choose a variety that shows some resistance to peach leaf curl.

Height/spread 13x13ft (4x4m) after 20 years

Life expectancy 20 years

Soil type Chalk, loam, sand; acid, alkaline, or neutral; moist but well-drained

Native to China

Hardiness Z 4–9

FIG

Ficus carica

Hailing from the Mediterranean, figs can be grown in cooler climates but need a bit of help. They do best in a very sheltered spot such as against a wall, away from prevailing wind, and they need well-drained soil. As well as providing fruit, figs are highly ornamental, with gorgeous gray bark and large, pale green three- to five-lobed leaves.

Fig trees can be fan-trained to grow flat against a sunny wall and also work well in pots—in fact, they seem to produce more fruit when their roots are slightly constricted. If you grow figs in the ground, constrict their growing space by burying vertical panel, such as corrugated iron or flagstones, around the rootball.

While most fig trees are hardy, some have been developed especially for a temperate climate. The cultivars 'Brown Turkey' and 'Brunswick' are particularly suitable. Figs can be dioecious, having both male and female flowers, which are unusually held within the fruit. But some fig cultivars available don't need pollination to fruit. Ripe figs are loved by blackbirds and some insects.

Some fig varieties rely on a small chalcid wasp to pollinate the flowers, which are inside the fruit. The female crawls into the fruit and lays her eggs, then her offspring grow within the flower, mate, and chew their way out. The wasps can become trapped and die, and the carnivorous fig fruit releases enzymes to break down the wasps' bodies and feed on them.

CARE NOTES

Transplant figs in pots every couple of years to a slightly larger pot—not too large, as figs do best with a smaller root run. Protect from harsh frost with horticultural fleece—smaller trees can be wrapped in a drawstring bag made of fleece. For fan-trained or large trees, drape over a couple of layers of fleece. After fall harvesting, you will be left with two types of figs: tiny pea-sized "embryo" fruit and larger, unripe figs. Remove the larger figs, as they will not ripen and will take energy away from the smaller fruits that will ripen the following year.

Height/spread 13x13ft (4x4m) after 20 years

Life expectancy 200 years

Soil type Chalk, loam, sand; alkaline or neutral; moist but well-drained

Native to Southern Europe, Asia

Hardiness Z 8–10

TREE PROFILES

ID NOTES

Leaves Large, leathery, and bright green with three to five lobes; yellow in fall

Twigs Olive-green with pointed leaf buds

Flowers Small and inconspicuous

Fruit Technically a bulbous stem containing clusters of seeds within

Bark Gray-brown, smooth

Leaf

Twig

Fruit

Flower

CITRUS

Citrus spp.

Oranges and lemons, along with limes and kumquats, are all part of the highly ornamental *Citrus* genus.

Citrus trees make fine garden plants in warmer areas and with climate change may thrive outdoors all year. However, it's currently best to grow them in pots that you can move indoors for winter. The fragrant flowers appear all year but are most prevalent in late winter. The fruit takes a year to mature, so flowers and fruit are often visible at the same time. Oranges tolerate a minimum winter night temperature of 50°F (10°C). Kumquats tolerate down to 45°F (7°C). The easiest, and hardiest, are lemons and Seville oranges. Limes need warmer temperatures than gardens in cooler areas offer.

ID NOTES

Leaves Glossy, oval, fresh green

Twigs Green, fading to brown

Flowers Extremely fragrant, five-petaled, white

Fruit Citrus fruits are edible specialized berries, known as hesperidiums; they vary in shape, color, and size but all have a peelable rind, known as a pericarp

Bark Dark brown

CARE NOTES

Citrus trees are hungry feeders, so need regular feeding with a proprietary citrus food. They can be prone to pests such as mealy bug and red spider mite, especially if grown in a conservatory or greenhouse.

Leaf

Twig

Flower

Citrus × limon

Height/spread Variable, up to 66ft (20m) after 20 years, but often smaller; about 5ft (1.5m) in a pot

Life expectancy 50 years

Soil type Chalk, loam, sand; alkaline or neutral; moist but well-drained

Native to Asia and Australia

Hardiness Z 9–11

MULBERRY

Morus nigra

Slow-growing, the mulberry can take seven years to start to produce but will then provide you with masses of delicious, sharp-tasting fruits for many years.

The fruits can be used in place of blackberries and raspberries in many recipes, including tarts and drinks. They make an excellent jam but are best eaten fresh with cream and sugar. Mulberries are excellent for wildlife—which means you'll have to share the fruit with blackbirds.

Mulberries are used in traditional Chinese medicines, where they are known as sang shen. They are a good source of iron and vitamin C. Plant compounds in mulberries have been linked to lower cholesterol and blood sugar and reducing the risk of cancer.

ID NOTES

Leaves Heart-shaped with downy undersides and faint toothed edges; yellow in fall

Twigs Thin and bendy with rounded, red-brown leaf buds

Flowers Insignificant and green

Fruit Blackberrylike with a sharp, acidic taste

Bark Gray-brown, rough, and grooved

CARE NOTES

Stake the mulberry when planting (see pp.148–149). Prune in winter to prevent sap from bleeding from the cuts, removing crossing, crowded, or damaged shoots (see pp.158–159).

Leaf

Flower

Fruit

Height/spread 39x26ft (12x8m) after 20 years

Life expectancy 100 years

Soil type Chalk, clay, loam, sand; acid, alkaline, or neutral; moist but well-drained

Native to Southwest Asia

Hardiness Z 5–10

BERRYING
TREES

Unsurprisingly, berrying trees are those that produce berries. While most aren't edible for humans, they are extremely valuable to wildlife, particularly birds. Some berries have extremely high levels of antioxidants, which help reduce the physical stresses of winter migration. Planting a berrying tree in your garden will provide an annual source of antioxidant-rich food for wildlife—and lots of color and interest for you too! While some berrying trees like holly have inconspicuous flowers, others like elder have beautiful flowers, giving them a long season of interest. Many are also suitable for hedging plants.

TREE PROFILES

ELDER

Sambucus nigra

A versatile plant with high wildlife value, elder can be grown as a tree or shrub or in a hedge.

Left unpruned, elder grows into a tall tree. In gardens, it can be cut back to keep it small, resulting in larger, more ornamental leaves (but sacrificing flowers and fruit). Its leaves are a caterpillar foodplant of many moth species, its flowers are loved by pollinators, and its berries eaten by birds. Insects hibernate in the crevices of its mature bark. The flowers can be used to make elderflower cordial or wine and the berries in jams, sauces, and other summer recipes. The berries have high levels of vitamin C. *Sambucus nigra* f. *porphyrophylla* 'Eva' (or 'Black Lace') has finely cut, almost black leaves; pink-flushed blooms; red-black berries; and red fall leaves.

Leaf

Berries

Flower

Height/spread 26x13ft (8x4m) after 20 years

Life expectancy 60 years

Soil type Chalk, clay, loam, sand; acid, alkaline, or neutral; moist but well-drained

Native to Europe, North Africa, southwest Asia

Hardiness Z 3–7

ID NOTES

Leaves Fresh green, pinnate with five to seven leaflets; red in fall in some species

Twigs Green, with an unpleasant smell

Flowers Flat umbels of cream, highly scented florets

Fruit/seed Purple-black berries borne in clusters

Bark Corky with deep crevices

CARE NOTES

Little routine care is needed. To keep your elder as a small shrub with larger leaves, prune it back annually when dormant to around 20in (50cm) above the ground—never prune beyond the point where the shrub starts to branch.

ID NOTES

Leaves Glossy, dark green, and oval; spiky when younger

Twigs Gray and fuzzy with blunt leaf buds

Flowers Inconspicuous, white with four petals

Fruit/seed Small red berries

Bark Smooth with "warts" or markings

Leaf

Twig and berries

Flower

TREE PROFILES

ENGLISH HOLLY

Ilex aquifolium

English holly is one of many species of holly across the world. It's a versatile evergreen shrub or small tree—grow it as a shrub or as part of a hedge or train it as a standard tree with a lollipop shape. Long used to decorate homes in winter, holly is associated with fertility. In traditional folklore, it's considered bad luck to cut down a holly tree.

English holly, along with other holly species, has excellent wildlife value. Its dense, prickly habit makes it a source of shelter for garden birds, its flowers are visited by bees and other pollinators, and its berries are eaten by birds and small mammals. Several butterfly and moth species, notably the holly blue butterfly, use holly as a caterpillar foodplant. Fallen leaves allowed to accumulate beneath a holly hedge may be used by overwintering animals. Male and female flowers appear on different plants. When buying holly, make sure you have a female plant, as it's only the female plants that bear berries. A male holly will be needed nearby to ensure pollination.

As well as the standard English holly, there are plenty of cultivars, some with different colored berries and/or variegated foliage. Some of the most appealing are *Ilex × altaclerensis* 'Golden King', which has gray-green leaves with a golden yellow margin and bright red berries, and *I. aquifolium* 'Bacciflava', which has yellow berries.

CARE NOTES

Holly needs very little care after planting, but keep it well watered for the first two years or so to help it establish. Pruning is just a matter of trimming to size in late winter or early spring—simply cut back those growing as a hedge or shrubs to keep them the desired shape. Remove lower branches of standard trees to maintain a clear trunk.

Height/spread 39x26ft (12x8m) after 20 years

Life expectancy 7 years, although some can live for up to 300 years

Soil type Chalk, clay, loam, sand; acid, alkaline, or neutral; moist but well-drained

Native to Western and southern Europe, northwest Africa, southwest Asia

Hardiness Z 5–9

MOUNTAIN ASH

Sorbus aucuparia

A fantastic tree, the mountain ash, or rowan, is typically associated
with high altitudes (as "mountain ash" suggests). Its leaves resemble those
of the ash tree, but that's where the similarities end. It makes an excellent
garden tree, being compact, excellent for wildlife, and providing
a long season of interest. Mountain ash trees can cope well with pollution,
so they are a good choice for urban areas.

From late spring, the mountain ash is covered in creamy blossom, while in fall it bears fantastic bright red berries, although these don't last long, as birds enjoy them so much. Vivid fall leaves add a final burst of color before the leaves fall. Traditionally grown to ward against witches, mountain ashes are now a popular tree to grow for wildlife.

There are many *Sorbus* species across the northern hemisphere, including some closely related ones, plus whitebeams and service trees. Many have been hybridized and some wonderful cultivars have resulted from them. *S.* 'Joseph Rock' is thought to be a natural hybrid—a botanist and explorer named Joseph Rock sent fruit and seeds from China to Edinburgh early in the 20th century, and a beautiful yellow-berried sorbus grew from one, although its heritage is unknown. As well as beautiful yellow berries, this cultivar also boasts incredible fall leaf color. All 'Joseph Rock' mountain ashes are grafted onto other *Sorbus* ash trees (see p.150), as they do not come true from seed.

CARE NOTES

Mountain ash trees are generally healthy and need little care. Remove dead and crossing stems as and when you need to (see pp.158–159) and water in very dry conditions. Grafted cultivars will produce suckers, which are new stems growing from the rootstock. Remove these when they're young either by rubbing them off by hand when they are buds or by trimming them back to the ground or stump if they are older.

Height/spread 39x26ft (12x8m) after 20 years

Life expectancy 100 years

Soil type Loam, sand; acid, neutral; moist but well-drained

Native to Europe, Asia

Hardiness Z 3–6

TREE PROFILES

ID NOTES

Leaves Pinnate, with up to eight pairs of leaflets plus a "terminal" leaflet at the end, each leaflet long, oval, and toothed; yellow in fall

Twigs Hairy, becoming smooth with age; leaf buds are large and purple and look like fat mittens

Flowers Five-petaled, cream, carried in dense clusters

Fruit/seed Dense clusters of bright red berries

Bark Smooth and silver-gray

Leaf

Twig

Flower

HAWTHORN

Crataegus monogyna

One of the best garden trees, hawthorn is compact and interesting to look at. It's an absolute magnet for wildlife—its leaves are a caterpillar foodplant for many species of moth; its flowers are visited by pollinating bees and flies; its berries are eaten by birds; and its gnarled, mature bark has crevices for hibernating insects. Mature trees provide nesting spots for birds, while a hawthorn hedge offers nesting opportunities for small mammals, too.

There are many species of hawthorn from various regions in the northern hemisphere. A number of cultivars have been bred from these, and you'll find double-flowered specimens that produce an even more impressive spring display. *Crataegus persimilis* 'Prunifolia' is more compact than *C. monogyna* and has more dramatic fall color.

Hawthorn has long been associated with the month of May, which it's sometimes named after. Its flowers have an unusual smell—in the Middle Ages, the flowers were said to smell of the Plague, and it was considered bad luck to bring hawthorn flowers into the home. Recent research has found that hawthorn flowers contain trimethylamine, a chemical also found in newly deceased bodies. The flowers really do, therefore, smell of the dead— presumably to attract insect pollinators, such as flies, to fertilize the blossom.

CARE NOTES

Hawthorns need very little care. Water well in the first two years after planting and trim shrubs and hedging plants into shape in fall. Remove crossing and dead branches from trees (see pp.158–159) and cut away lower branches from time to time when the tree is dormant to maintain a clear trunk.

Height/spread 26x26ft (8x8m) after 20 years

Life expectancy 150 years

Soil type Chalk, clay, loam, sand; acid, alkaline, or neutral; moist but well-drained

Native to Europe, North Africa, southwest Asia

Hardiness Z 3–9

ID NOTES

Leaves Small, fresh green, deeply lobed; yellow in fall

Twigs Slender, brown, and thorny

Flowers Strongly fragrant, five-petaled, white, and borne in clusters

Fruit/seed Red berries, known as haws

Bark Gray brown, maturing to develop fissures

Leaf

Berries

Twig

Flower

FLOWERING
TREES

All trees flower, but some trees' flowers are bigger and better than others, making them a perfect choice for a garden. Here, I've picked a selection with particularly lovely flowers, often without subsequent berries or fruit—but if you're after flowers and fruit, you'll also find beautiful flowering trees in the Fruit trees section (see pp.64–77). When buying flowering trees, it's worth checking to make sure they're suitable for pollinators. Sadly, not all flowering trees are—the flowers may be "double" (having extra petals at the expense of accessible pollen and nectar) or, if they're native to another country or region of the world, they could have the wrong shape for native pollinator mouths. Unless stated, all trees listed in this section have some value for pollinators.

CRAPE MYRTLE

Lagerstroemia indica

Flowering from late summer to fall, crape myrtles bear frilly flowers like crêpe paper in a range of colors, from pink and red to white.

Crape myrtle can be grown as a small tree or shrub, reaching 26ft (8m), but half that size is more likely in cooler climates. Insects love the flowers. A stalwart of North American and southern European city planting schemes, crape myrtles are rarely grown in cold climates, as they are hardy only to 23°F (-5°C) and don't reliably flower. That said, with climate change and a south-facing wall, you could consider growing one, as they put on quite a show. They can be grown in pots and moved indoors in winter, depending on size.

ID NOTES

Leaves Long, dark green, tinged with bronze when young; red, golden, and orange in fall

Twigs Straight, red-brown, with small leaf buds

Flowers Crêpelike, conical panicles in a range of colors

Fruit Clusters of upright seed capsules that remain throughout winter

Bark Peeling, gray-brown

CARE NOTES

Crape myrtles flower on the current season's growth, so annual hard pruning in winter promotes the best display. Simply cut the current season's growth back by half and remove suckers at the base on standard trees (but leave them for those grown as shrubs).

Leaf

Seed capsule

Height/spread 26x26ft (8x8m) after 20 years

Life expectancy 50 years

Soil type Chalk, loam, sand; acid, alkaline, or neutral; well-drained

Native to China, Korea

Hardiness Z 7–10

MAGNOLIA

Magnolia **spp.**

Iconic spring-flowering small trees or shrubs, magnolias bear tulip- or star-shaped flowers in pink or white, many with a strong fragrance. They can be deciduous or evergreen, and the different species range in size from 6½ft (2m) to 49ft (15m) high. The flowers of deciduous magnolias often appear before the leaves, making their spring display especially dramatic.

There's a magnolia for every garden, and it's worth spending time choosing the right one, as they're very slow-growing. Most require acid to neutral soil, but some will tolerate more alkaline soils, especially if it's enriched with an annual dressing of compost or manure. These include *Magnolia grandiflora*, *M. delavayi*, *M. kobus*, *M. × loebneri*, *M. stellata*, and *M. wilsonii*. Some smaller varieties, such as *M. stellata* 'Royal Star', *M. denudata* 'Sunrise', and *M.* 'George Henry Kern', can be grown in pots.

Always grow magnolias in a sheltered spot so frost doesn't spoil the look of the flowers.

M. stellata 'Jane Platt' is one of the best magnolias for a small garden, growing to an eventual height of just 10ft (3m). *M. grandiflora* is evergreen, offering year-round interest, but grows much taller, making it best for a larger space.

Magnolias have been around for millennia, since before bees, so their flowers are pollinated by beetles. A variety of beetles, including pollen beetles, will visit and pollinate magnolia flowers. While bees are still attracted to the pollen the flowers have on offer, they don't have a role in the fertilization of the flowers.

CARE NOTES

Magnolias do best in a rich soil, so mulch annually in spring with well-rotted manure or compost. They need little pruning, but if you want to shape yours or remove dead or damaged material (see pp.159–160), prune deciduous varieties from summer to fall and evergreen types in summer.

Height/spread From 6½x10ft (2x3m) to 49x33ft (15x10m) after 20 years

Life expectancy 100 years

Soil type Clay, loam, sand; acid, neutral; moist but well-drained

Native to Asia, the Americas and West Indies

Hardiness Z 7–10

Leaves Variable, typically green-golden, large and oval; golden yellow in fall in deciduous varieties

Twigs Brown, bendy with fat buds

Flowers Goblet- or star-shaped

Fruit/seed Clusters of fleshy fruit

Bark Brown and smooth

Leaf

Twig

Flower

ID NOTES

Leaves Oval, green, with prominent veining; some species have orange, red, or purple fall leaves

Twigs Slender, with opposite buds; brightly colored in some species

Flowers Variable; from clusters of small, inconspicuous flowers to large flowerlike bracts

Fruit/seed Small dark berries, elongated hiplike fruit, or rounded bumpy fruit

Bark Smooth and gray, aging to mottled and bumpy or peeling; or reddish, aging to mottled

Leaf

Twig

Flower

Cornus florida

DOGWOOD

Cornus spp.

The *Cornus* genus is a varied group of up to 60 species, and this diversity
means there's one for your garden. Flowering dogwoods, including
C. florida and *C. kousa,* are highly ornamental shrubs or small trees grown
for their colorful late-spring bracts (modified leaves that are larger and more
spectacular than the flowers). Shrubby dogwoods, including the British native
C. sanguinea, are grown for their colorful winter stems.

Flowering dogwoods are grown for their ornamental value over everything else. These include the beautiful *C. kousa* 'Miss Satomi', a pink-flowered dogwood, bearing masses of blooms in midsummer, and *C. florida*, which has huge, petal-like white bracts before its leaves unfurl and glorious fall color.

Want to grow a tree for wildlife? Choose *C. sanguinea* and leave it to grow into a hedge or small tree. If you wish to prune it hard to produce colorful winter color (see care notes, below), this will be at the expense of shrubby habitat, which many wild species need for shelter.

C. mas is a fantastic tree for small gardens, as it holds interest over a long season. From late winter, its bare branches are covered in clusters of small, bright yellow flowers, which are followed by cherrylike fruit (edible to people but also loved by birds). Its green leaves turn shades of yellow, red, and purple in fall.

CARE NOTES

Shrubby dogwoods (including *C. sanguinea*) do best in moist soil. For colorful winter stems, cut them to the ground in early spring, and the new growth stimulated by the pruning will be much brighter the following winter. Flowering dogwoods do much better in fertile, neutral to acidic soil and need very little pruning. Mulch all types annually in spring or fall.

Height/spread Varied, 10–26ft (3–8m), but most are pruned to keep growth in check

Life expectancy 70 years (flowering dogwoods); 80–100 years (shrubby dogwoods)

Soil type Chalk, clay, loam, sand; acid, alkaline, or neutral; moist but well-drained

Native to North America, parts of Europe, China, and Japan

Hardiness Z 5–9 (*C. florida*); Z 5–8 (other species)

LILAC

Syringa vulgaris

Popular in gardens, lilacs can be grown either as a shrub or a multistemmed small tree. They have extremely fragrant, star-shaped flowers, set off beautifully by fresh green leaves. It's thought that the color lilac was named after the shade of purple of the tree's flowers, although the flowers of some varieties actually come in a range of colors, including pink, purple, yellow, and white—not just lilac!

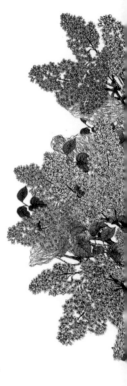

Lilac trees are particularly good for small gardens, as their flowers have a lovely fragrance and they're compact, so they'll never outgrow their space. They can be grown as multistemmed shrubs, or you can remove some of the lower branches to make more of a standard tree shape.

One of the best garden lilacs is *Syringa vulgaris* 'Sensation'. This bears masses of rich purple flowers with a cream margin and a strong fragrance, filling the air with scent. *S. vulgaris* 'Andenken an Ludwig Späth' has pink-purple flowers. "French lilac" trees are double-flowered cultivars that were bred by the French breeder Victor Lemoine in the 19th century.

Lilacs have been naturalized across North America and parts of Europe, but they are truly native to the rocky mountains of the Balkans.

CARE NOTES

Prune young plants to create an open framework and remove dead, crossing, or too-long branches (see pp.158–159). Very little pruning is needed on established trees; be careful when you do, as lilacs flower on the previous year's wood, so you risk losing some flowers. Late spring after flowering is the best time to prune.

Height/spread 13x13ft (4x4m) after 20 years

Life expectancy 50 years

Soil type Chalk, clay, loam, sand; acid, alkaline, or neutral; moist but well-drained

Native to Southeast Europe

Hardiness Z 3–7

ID NOTES

Leaves Heart-shaped, fresh green, and smooth, with prominent veining; green in fall

Twigs Brown with green leaf buds that turn purple in winter

Flowers Purple, star-shaped, in dense panicles, with a strong fragrance

Fruit/seed Brown seed capsules

Bark Gray-brown, smooth when young, maturing to flaky

Leaf

Twig

Seed capsule

EVERGREEN
TREES

Evergreen trees are useful in small gardens, as they provide
winter interest when other trees are dormant and leafless.
But it's not just in winter that evergreens stand out—many
have beautiful flowers and fruit at other times of the year,
while others provide a solid green backdrop for more
colorful plants. You'll have noticed a few evergreen trees
in other sections, but here's a good selection of trees
renowned for their evergreen beauty.

MEDITERRANEAN CYPRESS

Cupressus sempervirens

Popular with garden designers, the Mediterranean (or Italian or Tuscan) cypress is an elegant conifer that grows tall and slender.

In a large garden, grow cypress trees in a row where they can form an impressive backdrop to the rest of your garden, which you can then balance with more rounded shapes. A row can be used to line an entrance or mark a boundary or to make a sophisticated architectural statement. In a small garden, just one or two trees can provide an evergreen "accent" to a border or gravel garden. Choose a sunny, sheltered site with well-drained soil. In the Mediterranean, this evergreen is known as the "drama tree" because it has a tendency to bend at the slightest breeze.

Height/spread 39x13ft (12x4m) after 20–50 years

Life expectancy 500 years

Soil type Chalk, clay, loam, sand; acid, alkaline, or neutral; well-drained

Native to Mediterranean

Hardiness Z 7–10

Bark

Cone

Leaf

ID NOTES

Leaves Dense sprays of gray-green foliage

Twigs Red-brown

Cones Small, ¾–1¼in (2–3cm) in diameter

Bark Red-brown with vertical ridges, aging to gray

CARE NOTES

No pruning is required, but you may want to remove the odd branch growing in the wrong direction. Brown patches may be caused by cypress aphid (*Cinara cupressivora*), found in summer, or Coryneum canker, caused by a fungus and resulting in branch dieback. Most brown patches will heal naturally, while branch dieback can be pruned out. Encourage birds into your garden to keep aphids at bay.

ENGLISH PRIVET

Ligustrum vulgare

A semievergreen shrub, occasionally forming a multibranched tree, English privet has spectacular summer flowers. It's commonly found in hedgerows and on the edges of woodland, as well as scrubby grassland. In gardens, it makes an excellent hedging plant, although has a slightly wilder growing habit than the more commonly used Chinese privet (*Ligustrum ovalifolium*).

Sadly, English privet is usually trimmed before the creamy-white flowers emerge, especially when it's part of a hedge. If you leave them to grow, you'll be rewarded with masses of bees, as privet flowers are a bee magnet. These flowers are followed by small, dark berries, which are poisonous to humans but popular with a number of garden birds.

It's the main foodplant of the privet hawk moth and a few other moth species and provides shelter for small birds and mammals.
Privet will grow almost anywhere and can cope with sea winds; full sun; partial shade; and light, dry soil, as well as sandy conditions. The only thing it doesn't do well in is boggy soil.

CARE NOTES

Keep young plants watered and weed-free for two years after planting. Prune hedges annually (see pp.158–160), ideally in winter after berrying, so that the bees and birds can make the most of its flowers and fruit. By this time of year, there will be no danger of disturbing nesting birds either. Stunted growth and yellow leaves are a sign of boggy soil, and efforts should be made to improve drainage, such as digging around the plants and adding gravel.

Height/spread 13x13ft (4x4m), but is usually clipped as a hedge

Life expectancy 50 years

Soil type Chalk, clay, loam, sand; acid, alkaline, or neutral; moist but well-drained

Native to Europe, including the British Isles

Hardiness Z 6–8

ID NOTES

Leaves Oval, glossy, and dark green with a central rib

Twigs Gray-brown with alternate buds

Flower Cream, lilaclike panicles

Fruit/seed Small black, poisonous berries

Bark Gray-brown and smooth

Flower

Fruit

ID NOTES

Leaves Oblong, glossy, and green with a paler central rib

Twigs Red-brown, smooth

Flowers Urn-shaped, white with a pink flush

Fruit/seed Round, strawberrylike

Bark Rusty brown and peeling

Leaf

Fruit

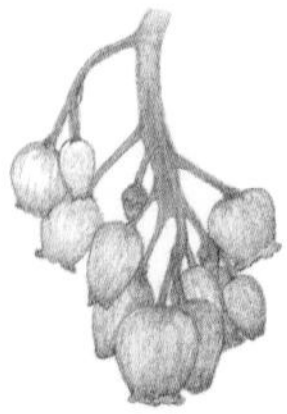

Flower

STRAWBERRY TREE

Arbutus unedo

The strawberry tree bears delicate, urn-shaped flowers and at the same
time strawberrylike fruit, giving it the common name of strawberry
tree. All these features make it a beautiful choice for a garden tree.
Its evergreen, baylike leaves take the strawberry tree's ornamental
value through into winter.

A magnificent sight, the strawberry tree is native to the Mediterranean, where it grows among cork trees and craggy hilltops in the driest soils. It's also native to Ireland but not the rest of the British Isles. Hardy down to 14°F (-10°C), it can be grown in many different areas of the US.

Tolerant of pollution and salt, the strawberry tree thrives both in cities and coastal gardens. It doesn't grow too big, so it makes an excellent choice for a small garden. Its urn-shaped flowers are popular with bees and its fruit is loved by birds. (The fruit is also edible for humans, but not particularly tasty.)

The variety 'Compacta' grows to a maximum height and spread of just 8ft (2.5m) and is suitable for growing in a pot.

CARE NOTES

Young plants may need protection from hard frosts—simply drape with a couple of layers of horticultural fleece or move pot-grown plants under cover. Cold winds can cause leaf scorch. Fungal leaf spot disease can affect strawberry trees. This disease is usually nothing to worry about but can cause leaf drop and loss of vigor. Remove and burn infected leaves. Avoid pruning, unless it's to remove damaged or crossing stems. Mulch in fall.

Height/spread 26x26ft (8x8m) after 20 years

Life expectancy 400 years

Soil type Loam, sand; acid, alkaline, or neutral; moist but well-drained

Native to Mediterranean, northwest Europe, and Ireland

Hardiness Z 7–10

SEED- AND NUT-BEARING TREES

Seeds and nuts are invaluable to wildlife, and many are edible for people, too. Plant a seed- or nut-bearing tree and the wildlife will visit your garden for years. Squirrels and large birds such as woodpeckers may come looking for acorns and pine cones, while smaller birds such as blue jays may gather beechnuts and seeds. Bear in mind that any seeds and nuts that fall to the ground will try to germinate. Squirrels and some birds, too, will bury the seeds and forget about them, resulting in free tree seedlings for you and your neighbors!

SPINDLE

Euonymus europaeus

In fall, spindle's leaves turn glorious shades of red and orange before falling to reveal pink fruits with bright orange seeds, which persist into winter.

A small tree, spindle can reach 30ft (9m) but is more likely to reach about 13ft (4m). It can be a great option for attracting wildlife—its flowers are pollinated by insects and its seeds eaten by birds. The leaves feed caterpillars of several moth species, including the magpie, spindle ermine, and scorched moths, as well as the holly blue butterfly. Aphids flock to spindle leaves in spring and summer, providing birds with a much-needed source of natural food. Be careful around children and pets—all parts of spindle can cause discomfort if ingested. Wear gloves and wash hands after touching it.

Leaf

Twig

Seeds

Height/spread 30x13ft (9x4m) after 10–20 years

Life expectancy 150 years

Soil type Chalk, clay loam, sand; acid, alkaline, or neutral; moist but well-drained

Native to Europe, Asia

Hardiness Z 3–7

ID NOTES

Leaves Oval, fresh green; red and orange in fall

Twigs Deep green when young, thin, and straight

Flowers Small white/yellow, in panicles

Fruit/seed Pink fruit cases that split to reveal bright orange seeds

Bark Deep green, fading to brown and developing corky fissures with age

CARE NOTES

Spindle is relatively trouble free. There's no need to prune unless you want to reduce its size. If you do need to prune, do so in spring or fall. Avoid waterlogged areas.

ID NOTES

Leaves Rounded, fresh green, and never pointed; orange and yellow in fall

Twigs Spotted with an orange/red tip; sticky

Flowers Conelike female catkins and tassel-like male catkins

Fruit/seed Borne in tiny brown female catkins that look like cones and stay on the tree throughout winter

Bark Dark, fissured

Female catkins

Twig

Male catkins

ALDER

Alnus glutinosa

Strongly associated with wetter habitats, the alder is a wonderful European tree that's often found in wet woodland or "carrs" with other moisture-tolerant trees, such as silver birch. It has a conical shape and gently rustling leaves, making it a fine choice for a large garden. Alder can also be grown as a hedge and is particularly useful for waterlogged or boggy gardens.

Alder is the foodplant for several moth caterpillars, including the wonderfully named alder kitten. In spring, its male catkins offer early pollen for bees. However, they are actually wind-pollinated and, once pollinated, the female catkins grow woody and resemble tiny pine cones. These open in fall to release their flat, waxy seeds, which have two corky wings to help them float on water and disperse to new ground. The remaining seeds are eaten by siskins, redpolls, and goldfinches—alder seed is the main source of winter food for the siskin, which extracts it by reaching far into the crevices of the catkin with its long, slim bill.

Below ground, it has a strong relationship with the bacterium *Frankia alni*, which forms nodules on its roots. The nodules absorb nitrogen from the air, making it available to the tree. In return, the alder provides the bacteria with carbon. This enables the alder to grow on poor soils and improves the soil.

When cut, alder wood turns bright orange. Alder trees have long been regarded with suspicion, and in Ireland, it was considered bad luck to pass an alder.

CARE NOTES

Alder needs moist soil to thrive. Pruning is rarely necessary, although you may want to remove crossing or dead stems (see pp.158–159) in late spring to summer. Alder is prone to alder sucker, a sap-sucking bug with nymphs that are covered in white, waxy threads. These can be quite noticeable but rarely cause damage to the tree.

Height/spread 82x26ft (25x8m) after 15–20 years

Life expectancy 60 years

Soil type Chalk, clay, loam, sand; acid, alkaline, or neutral; moist but well-drained

Native to Europe, southwest Asia, and northern Africa

Hardiness Z 3–7

HAZEL

Corylus avellana

A lovely small tree and brilliantly versatile, hazel can be grown as a multistemmed shrub, standard tree, as part of a hedge, or coppiced. Its fresh green leaves and multistemmed habit make hazel a perfect choice for a woodland border while, if grown as a small tree or shrub, it has a lovely shape. It's fast growing and will quickly fill its space.

Both male and female flowers appear on the same tree. Male flowers are long, yellow catkins, while female flowers are tiny—look for fine red styles or threads protruding from a green bud, usually at the top of a cluster of male catkins. Hazel is wind pollinated, but the male catkins also provide pollen for early bees. Hazel is a useful habitat for many other wild species, including the caterpillars of the large emerald and small white wave, barred umber, and nut-tree tussock moths. A large number of birds and mammals enthusiastically consume its nuts, including the aptly named hazel dormouse.

Hazel has long been associated with coppicing—a traditional way of managing woodland. Young stems are cut close to the ground to promote growth of new shoots. These shoots are harvested after a few years, starting the cycle again. Coppicing brings light to the woodland floor, allowing spring flowers to bloom while providing fuel and young, straight stems for walking sticks, bean poles, and basket weaving.

CARE NOTES

Very little care is needed if you leave your hazel to grow naturally. If you want to coppice your tree to manage its size or even to use its stems in the garden, simply cut back all the stems to around 2in (5cm) from the ground in February or March. Repeat every few years once strong new shoots have formed. Trim hazel hedges in late winter before growth starts in spring. Never let the soil around hazel dry out completely—water in very dry weather if there is a long dry spell.

Height/spread 26x26ft (8x8m) but often smaller if clipped as a hedge or coppiced

Life expectancy 80 years, longer if coppiced

Soil type Chalk, loam, sand; alkaline or neutral; moist but well-drained

Native to Europe, including the British Isles

Hardiness Z 4–8

ID NOTES

Leaves Heart-shaped, ribbed and toothed, fresh green, and soft with hairs on the underside; yellow in fall

Twigs Bendy and hairy

Flowers Male catkins like lambs' tails and bright red, stringlike female flowers on the same plant, appearing in late winter

Fruit/seed Edible nuts encased in a leafy husk

Bark Smooth, gray-brown, peels with age

Leaf

Nuts

Female flower

Male catkins

ID NOTES

Leaves Oval, pale green with slightly hairy undersides

Twigs Red-brown to green

Flowers Large fluffy yellow catkins before the leaves burst

Fruit/seed Small capsules, each containing seeds encased in white fluff

Bark Smooth, gray

Leaf

Catkins

Salix caprea 'Kilmarnock'

KILMARNOCK WILLOW

Salix caprea 'Kilmarnock'

There are around 400 types of willow trees in the *Salix* genus. Many are enormous and far too big to grow in the average garden; you'll find them along riverbanks, where they thrive in the damp soil. But the Kilmarnock willow is a notable exception and has many beautiful features that make it a dream for a smaller garden.

Technically, a pussy willow grafted onto another willow species, the Kilmarnock willow has a weeping habit. It will never grow more than 8ft (2.5m) tall and provides much of the wildlife value of larger willows, but in a small space. Grow it in a sunny spot, where it will put on the best display of catkins. Several species of moth use it, while bumblebees, solitary bees, and some species of fly flock to it for the pollen- and nectar-rich catkins in early spring. It's a hugely important source of food for pollinators, as it flowers earlier than many other spring-flowering plants.

Another willow suitable for smaller gardens is *S. alba* var. *vitellina* 'Britzensis'. While its parent, *S. alba*, grows to 82ft (25m) tall or more and needs wet soil to thrive, 'Britzensis' is cultivated for garden use, tolerating clay and damp sites but not dry ones. It is usually cut in early spring to make the most of its bright red shoots, which are more colorful when young. It's ideal for the winter garden.

CARE NOTES

Water regularly for the first couple of years. Otherwise, little care is needed apart from removing dead or damaged stems (see pp.158–159). Older trees may need thinning as growth becomes congested. To do this, remove whole stems back to the main framework of branches in spring—avoid shortening stems part of the way, as this will encourage lots of shoots and make congestion worse, and you could end up with a very unnatural-looking tree that appears to have had a severe haircut. To prune the variety 'Britzensis' for its bright, young shoots, cut shoots in late winter or spring to 2–3in (5–8cm) from the ground, then repeat annually or every few years, cutting to the previous stubs.

Height/spread 6x8ft (1.8x2.5m) after 20 years

Life expectancy 50 years

Soil type Clay, loam, sand; acid, alkaline, or neutral; moist but well-drained

Native to Temperate regions of Europe and North America

Hardiness Z 4–8

SILVER BIRCH

Betula pendula

A beautiful, deciduous tree with a conical shape, silver birch grows to 66ft (20m). Unlike many trees, its height isn't imposing, as it has a light canopy—letting sunlight filter through its gently weeping branches—and small leaves. It has elegant, peeling white bark, which develops dark, diamond-shaped fissures with age. In fall, its leaves turn a gorgeous, buttery yellow before falling.

Popular with wildlife, silver birch is loved by goldfinches, which grab the seeds with their beaks and hold them against a branch with their toes while feasting. Redpolls and pine siskins eat its seeds, too. It tolerates pollution, making it a good choice for city gardens.

In spring, as the tree starts to come into leaf, you can press your ear against a bare section of trunk and listen to the sap rising in the tree. It's said to sound like a fast-flowing river. The sap (often called birch water) has been consumed by people for centuries straight from the tree; it is nutrient rich and believed to have many medicinal properties. To "tap" a birch for its sap, choose one with a trunk diameter of 10in (25cm) and drill a hole in the trunk 1in (3cm) deep and about 3ft (1m) from the ground, in an upward-facing direction. Use a piece of tubing or similar to direct the sap into a container. Avoid tapping the tree every year—give it a couple of years' rest between tapping.

Other birches that make good garden trees include the ornamental Himalayan birch (*B. utilis*) and the Chinese red birch (*B. albosinensis*).

CARE NOTES

Very little care is needed, although formative pruning in fall or winter may be necessary to remove lower branches if you want a single-stemmed tree (see pp.157–158). Don't allow the soil to dry out—mulching annually will help conserve soil moisture.

Height/spread 65x26ft (20x8m) after 50 years

Life expectancy 80 years

Soil type Chalk, clay, loam, sand; acid, alkaline, or neutral; moist but well-drained

Native to Europe and Asia, including the British Isles

Hardiness Z 2–7

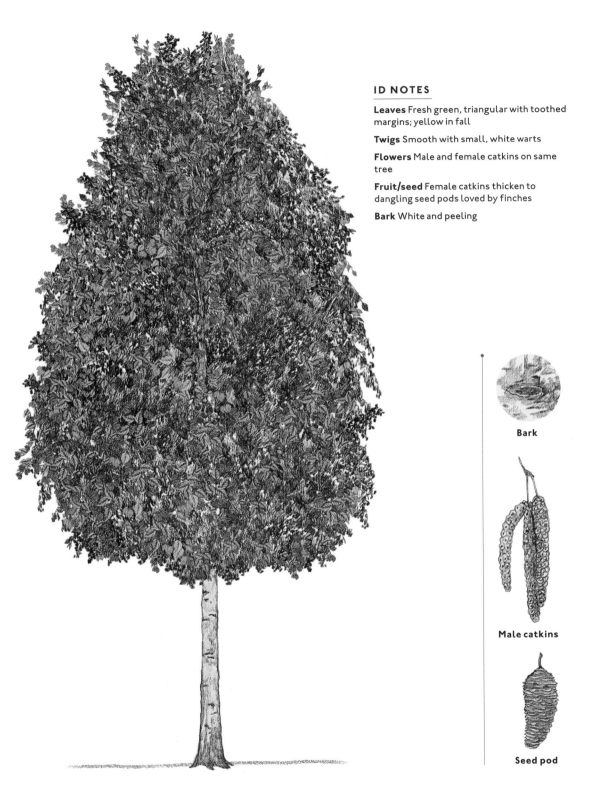

ID NOTES

Leaves Fresh green, triangular with toothed margins; yellow in fall

Twigs Smooth with small, white warts

Flowers Male and female catkins on same tree

Fruit/seed Female catkins thicken to dangling seed pods loved by finches

Bark White and peeling

Bark

Male catkins

Seed pod

Seed- and nut-bearing trees

ID NOTES

Leaves Oblong, glossy, and with parallel veins; yellow in fall

Twigs Purple-brown with oval, plum-colored buds

Flowers Male and female catkins are long and yellow and found on the same tree

Fruit/seed Sweet chestnuts wrapped in a prickly husk known as a burr

Bark Gray-purple and smooth, develops deep grooves with age

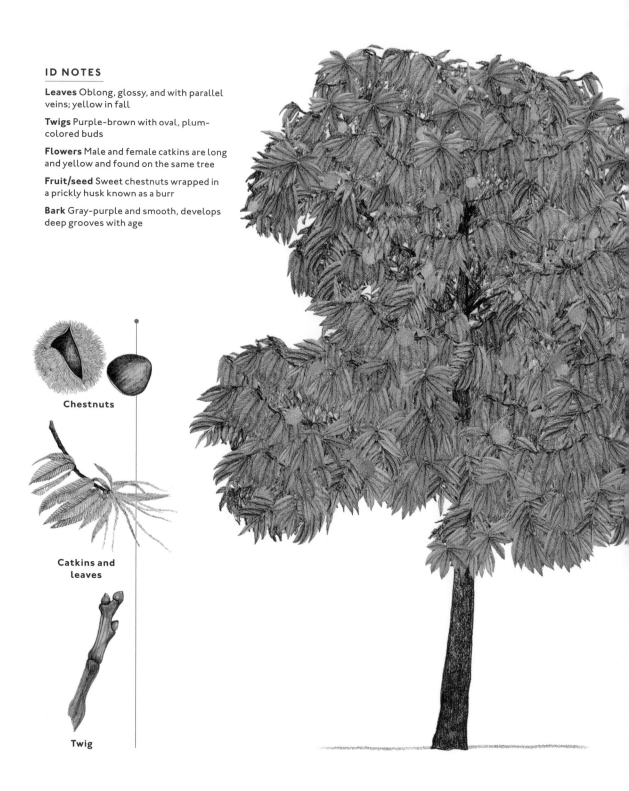

Chestnuts

Catkins and leaves

Twig

TREE PROFILES

SWEET CHESTNUT

Castanea sativa

Related to oaks and beeches, the sweet chestnut is a large deciduous tree, suitable only for large gardens. It's a majestic-looking tree, with smooth gray-purple bark that develops deep ridges with age. The best thing about it, though, is its chestnuts, which are traditionally roasted on "an open fire" at Christmas.

Each spiky chestnut case holds two to three chestnuts, which are smaller and lighter brown than the inedible horse chestnut, *Aesculus hippocastanum* (see pp.120–121). The flowers are visited by pollinators in spring, while squirrels eat the nuts. Several species of moth use its leaves as a foodplant.

The sweet chestnut was introduced to Britain by the Romans, who used the nuts to make a sort of oatmeal. In London's Greenwich Park, there are 52 sweet chestnut trees thought to date back to the mid-1600s.

Harvest sweet chestnuts in October when they drop from the tree, the burrs (outer spiny skins) bursting and the nuts spilling out as they land. Some need removing from their skin—you may want to wear thick gloves for this, as the burrs are very spiny. Either freeze them or eat them as soon as you have harvested them, as they dry out quickly. They can be eaten raw (when they're crunchy) or roasted, which softens them. They are also used in stuffing mixtures and in stews, soups, and more substantial meals.

CARE NOTES

Choose a sunny spot to ensure the maximum number of nuts are produced. Bear in mind that trees may take 20 years to bear fruit—though some varieties, such as 'Marron de Lyon', will bear fruit after just two or three years. Water well until it becomes established and mulch annually with well-rotted manure or compost.

Height/spread 115x33ft (35x10m) after 50 years

Life expectancy 600 years

Soil type Loam, sand; acid or neutral; well-drained

Native to Southern Europe and parts of Asia

Hardiness Z 5–7

ALMOND

Prunus dulcis

Almonds make fantastic ornamental trees, with gorgeous, soft pink spring blossom. They have been cultivated for thousands of years. The tree was introduced to California in the 1800s, and the state now produces some 80 percent of the world's almonds, although there are serious concerns as to the sustainability of almond production in California owing to the severe droughts experienced there in recent years—almonds are thirsty trees.

In colder climates, almonds are unlikely to bear fruit, as their early flowers are susceptible to spring frosts. They do best where winters are mild and summers are hot. However, there are almond trees that do well in the urban heat islands of large cities and that do bear fruit (and therefore almonds). Unless you choose a self-fertile variety such as 'Robijn', you'll need a male and female tree for any chance of success.

But they are worth it for the blossom alone, and you never know—you may be lucky with fruit. Grow your almond in a very sheltered, sunny spot, as you would a peach or nectarine.

The fragrant almond nuts are used in baking; confectionery; and "mylk," a milklike liquid made from blending soaked almonds. Oil from the nut is used in cosmetics.

CARE NOTES

Choose a St. Julien or Montclair rootstock for a maximum height of around 15ft (4.5m). Pruning takes place in late summer and is not dissimilar to that of apple trees—after planting, cut back branches by one-third to promote a bushy shape. Over time, prune to create an open center so that light and air can reach the developing fruits (see pp.160–161). Trees may be susceptible to leaf curl—the only way to manage this is to pick off and destroy infected leaves in spring. Keep young trees well watered in dry periods.

Height/spread 26x13ft (8x4m) after 20–50 years

Life expectancy 50 years

Soil type Chalk, clay, loam, sand; acid, alkaline, or neutral; moist but well-drained

Native to Iran and surrounding countries

Hardiness Z 7–9

ID NOTES

Leaves Oblong, with prominent veining; yellow in fall

Twigs Gray and smooth with alternate, reddish flower buds

Flowers Bright pink, star-shaped

Fruit/seed Oblong, furry-textured case containing an almond

Bark Gray-brown and fissured

Nuts

Flower

Seed- and nut-bearing trees

LARGE
TREES

Suitable only for large gardens, this selection of trees consists
mostly of British deciduous trees, such as oak, beech, and
linden. They're absolutely worth growing if you have the
space but need some careful planning as to where they will
live. The largest trees range in height from 66ft (20m) to
some 148ft (45m), with the spread of the tree sometimes
eventually matching its height. They take time to mature,
and you'll never see your tree reach its final height and
spread, but many generations will enjoy it—some large
trees can live for over 1,000 years!

YEW

Taxus baccata

Often found in British churchyards, yew is a coniferous tree that can become enormous, it but also makes a fine hedging and topiary plant.

Yews can be grown as single- or multi-stemmed trees, providing year-round, evergreen interest for us; flowers for pollinators; and bright red berries for birds and small mammals. All parts are toxic to humans, but particularly the seeds, and should not be eaten. Birds and mammals can pass the seeds through their digestive system without being harmed. Grown as a hedge or large topiary form, yew offers a green foil for colorful plants. Its dense foliage helps hide unsightly views and provides nesting for birds. Yew is one of Europe's longest-lived plants.

Height/spread 49ft (15m) after 20–50 years

Life expectancy 3,000 years

Soil type Loam, chalk, clay, sand; acid or neutral; well-drained

Native to Europe and North Africa

Hardiness Z 6–8

Fruit

Flower

ID NOTES

Leaves Dark green, pointed needles

Twigs Dark green

Flowers Male and female flowers grow on different trees in spring; male flowers off-white, small, and round; female flowers look like green, scaly buds

Fruit/seed Small red drupe containing one hard seed

Bark Reddish-brown, fissured, and peeling

CARE NOTES

Water well as yew establishes, then you won't need to water it again. Yew needs very little care and no pruning. However, topiary and hedges need regular trimming to form and maintain size and shape (see pp.158–160).

ID NOTES

Leaves Fresh green, oval in shape, and ribbed; yellow/orange in fall

Twigs Slender and gray with alternate, torpedo-shaped buds

Flowers Insignificant, rounded catkins; the male catkin is slightly smaller and darker

Fruit/seed Beech "mast" forms as small, hard-shelled fruit with a spiky surface and angled, glossy brown seeds inside

Bark Smooth and gray

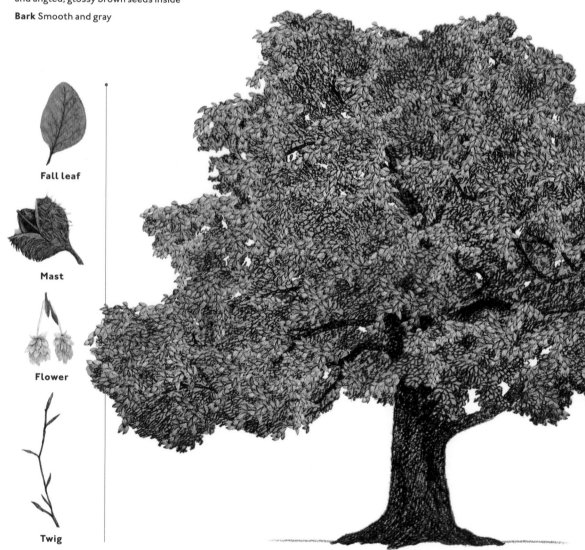

Fall leaf

Mast

Flower

Twig

EUROPEAN BEECH

Fagus sylvatica

European beech is one of the most beautiful woodland trees. Its fresh, green, slightly hairy leaves mark spring before aging to a darker green and losing their furry coat. They develop an orangey hue with age and then turn a glorious russet before dropping in fall. The smooth, gray bark is the perfect foil for all this leafy beauty.

Beech trees are excellent for wildlife: their leaves are eaten by the caterpillars of several species of moth and the mast (seeds) are eaten by mice, voles, squirrels, and birds. As they age, they provide homes for nesting birds and squirrels, and the bark is often home to fungi, mosses, and lichens. Mature trees shed masses of leaves in fall that are perfect for making leaf mold. The mast root readily into pots and garden borders.

If you love beech trees but don't have space for a tree, then a beech hedge could be a good option for you. Young beech trees hold onto their leaves in winter, and the pruning process keeps hedges in their juvenile state so they retain their leaves all year round, forming a really effective screen even in winter. Beech hedges are things of beauty—formal yet soft, with the winter leaves ensuring they look good all year.

CARE NOTES

Keep well watered for the first couple of years after planting. Beech trees need very little care, but hedges need regular pruning (see pp.158–160). Formative pruning should be done in winter but, once established, prune in late summer (after birds have finished nesting). Taper hedges slightly so the base is wider than the top—this ensures light reaches all parts of the hedge.

Height/spread 131x66ft (40x20m) after 20–50 years

Life expectancy 600 years

Soil type Chalk, clay, loam, sand; acid, alkaline, or neutral; moist but well-drained

Native to Europe and the southeast of the British Isles

Hardiness Z 4–7

ENGLISH OAK

Quercus robur

Our common oak, known as English oak, is one of two native British species of oak (and the more dominant of the two). A further three species have been naturalized in the British Isles, and there are about 600 around the world. Related to the beech, the English oak is a large, majestic tree, with characteristic lobed leaves and acorn fruits.

The English oak supports more life than any other British tree species, including hundreds of types of insects, which in turn are food for birds and their young, plus mammals and other insects. Birds such as jays feast on its acorns, while holes and crevices in the bark are used by other birds, bats, and squirrels. The English oak is host to fungi such as fly agaric, cep, and chicken of the woods. Its rotting leaves offer opportunities for detritivores such as centipedes, beetles, caterpillars, and even mammals.

Oaks can on occasion live for up to 1,000 years. As they age, their crown starts to die back, allowing light to reach the inner crown, which stimulates growth and eventually results in a new, smaller crown developing. The old branches die off but can remain on the tree, giving the tree a "stag-headed" appearance.

Fantastic garden trees, oaks are suitable only for very large gardens. Plant an oak and think of those who will enjoy it in 200; 500; and even 1,000 years' time.

CARE NOTES

An oak tree needs little care after planting, but water it regularly in its first two years. You can expect your English oak to grow to around 33 ft (10m) tall after 20 years, and it will only start producing acorns after this time.

Height/spread 115x33ft (35x10m) after 50 years

Life expectancy 1,000 years

Soil type Chalk, clay loam, sand; acid, alkaline, or neutral; moist but well-drained

Native to Temperate regions of Europe and North America

Hardiness Z 5–8

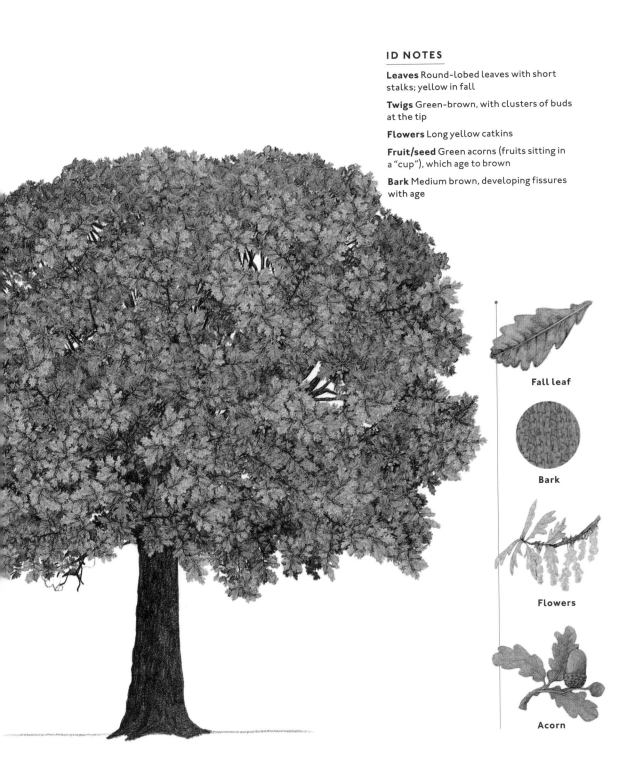

ID NOTES

Leaves Round-lobed leaves with short stalks; yellow in fall

Twigs Green-brown, with clusters of buds at the tip

Flowers Long yellow catkins

Fruit/seed Green acorns (fruits sitting in a "cup"), which age to brown

Bark Medium brown, developing fissures with age

Fall leaf

Bark

Flowers

Acorn

Large trees

ID NOTES

Leaves Palmate, with five to seven oval, ribbed leaflets; red/brown in fall

Twigs Red-brown with sticky, rounded buds

Flowers Candlelike spires of individual white florets, tinged pink

Seeds Hard conker encased in a spiky green shell

Bark Smooth, pink-gray when young, developing fissures with age

Fall leaf

Twig

Conker

HORSE CHESTNUT

Aesculus hippocastanum

The horse chestnut, or conker tree, is a stalwart of children's storybooks and playground history. Its conkers have been used in conker fights for generations, with children seeking out the biggest, shiniest conkers; forcing holes into them; and looping string through them so they could bash each other with them during recess—now a practice discouraged in schools.

Conker trees are a thing of beauty. Tall and majestic, their fresh green leaves and candelabralike flowers mark the coming of spring, while their conkers tell us that fall has arrived. When the leaves fall during the season, they leave a scar on the twig they detached from, which resembles an inverted horseshoe complete with nail holes, giving the tree its common name.

While it is native to the Balkans, the horse chestnut is considered naturalized to the British Isles. Its flowers are visited by a number of pollinators, and a couple of moths use its leaves as a caterpillar foodplant. Large mammals eat the conkers.

In recent years, the horse chestnut has been affected by the horse chestnut leaf mining moth, a southern European species first found in Britain in 2002. It lays its eggs on the leaves and its larvae mine inside, eating them from within. Brown or white blotches are visible on the leaves. Heavily affected trees can drop leaves early, but this appears not to affect its vigor. Some birds eat the larvae and their cocoons, so could provide some long-term natural control for the moth.

CARE NOTES

Very little care is needed beyond formative pruning, where crossing, dead, and low-growing branches should be removed (see pp.158–159). Water for the first two years when conditions are dry.

Height/spread 131x66ft (40x20m) after 20–50 years

Life expectancy 300 years

Soil type Loam, sand; acid or neutral; moist but well-drained

Native to The Balkans

Hardiness Z 3–8

SMALL-LEAVED LINDEN

Tilia cordata

The small-leaved linden is a huge deciduous tree, suitable only for large gardens. That said, it's a wonderful specimen if you do have a large garden. Its fresh green leaves make the perfect spring spectacle; its fragrant flowers attract bees; and its leaves are used by a range of moths, including the gorgeous lime hawk moth.

Because small-leaved linden trees are so long-lived, they provide dead wood for wood-boring beetles and nesting holes for birds. Aphids are attracted to linden trees, providing a source of food for birds and insect predators such as hoverflies and ladybugs. Bees even drink aphid honeydew from the leaves in spring. Beware: honeydew from aphids can be an issue, and anything beneath your linden tree—such as a car or garden furniture—could have a dressing of honeydew before long!

Linden trees have a gruesome, slightly macabre relationship with bees, in that the nectar of some species, particularly the silver linden (*Tilia tomentosa*), is thought to kill them. For years, dead bees (usually bumblebees) have been observed beneath linden trees. It's thought the nectar in the flowers is toxic to bees. It's not fully understood how or why this happens. Some have suggested that, in a dry spring, certain compounds are more concentrated in the nectar, making it more toxic. Small-leaved linden isn't considered to be one of the dangerous lindens to bees, so consider it a bee-friendly tree for a large garden. But keep it well watered, just in case!

CARE NOTES

Water in dry periods. Formative prune young trees by removing crossing, dead, and low-growing branches (see pp.158–159). It will take 20–50 years to reach its maximum height, depending on growing conditions.

Height/spread 82x66ft (25x20m) after 50 years

Life expectancy 200 years

Soil type Chalk, clay, sand; alkaline or neutral; moist but well-drained

Native to Europe

Hardiness Z 3–8

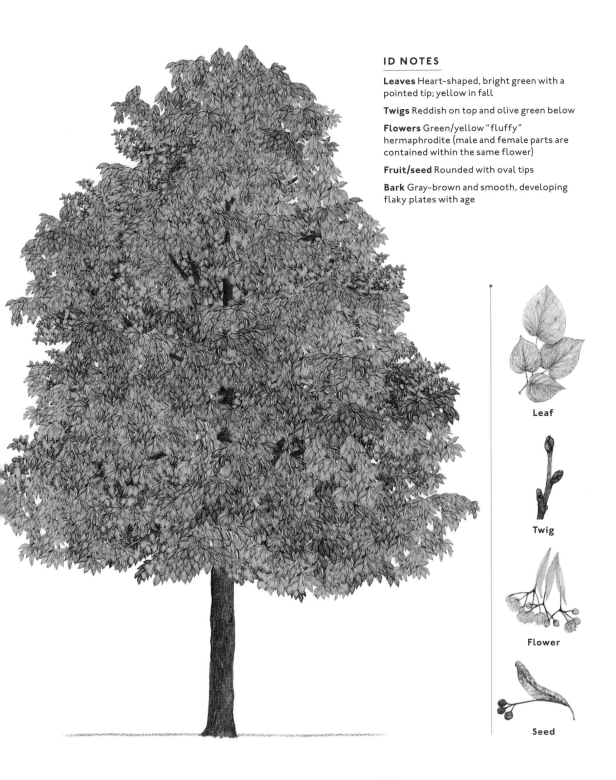

ID NOTES

Leaves Heart-shaped, bright green with a pointed tip; yellow in fall

Twigs Reddish on top and olive green below

Flowers Green/yellow "fluffy" hermaphrodite (male and female parts are contained within the same flower)

Fruit/seed Rounded with oval tips

Bark Gray-brown and smooth, developing flaky plates with age

Leaf

Twig

Flower

Seed

TREES FOR
FALL COLOR

The leaves of many deciduous trees change color before
falling during fall (see pp.42–43), but some look truly
spectacular. So if you're looking for a tree that wows in fall,
look no further. Inevitably, as in other categories
in this book, this list of trees isn't exhaustive, and you'll find
trees in other parts of the book with excellent fall color.
(Cherry trees, in the Fruit tree section, and beech, in the
Large trees section, both look glorious as their leaves turn.)
However, this section is made up of trees that are particularly
known for their fall leaf coloring, such as the wonderful
sweet gum and Japanese maple.

Cercis canadensis
'Forest Pansy'

Height/spread 16x16ft (5x5m) after 20 years

Life expectancy 70 years

Soil type Loam, sand; acid or neutral; moist but well-drained

Native to North America

Hardiness Z 5–9

Twig

Flower

REDBUD

Cercis canadensis

A gorgeous tree for a small garden, redbud is native to eastern North America, including Canada. The species has beautiful heart-shaped leaves and pink, pealike flowers.

Arguably the best garden variety is 'Forest Pansy'. Its flowers appear in spring on bare wood, followed by bright red, heart-shaped leaves that darken to a lustrous purple. In fall, the leaves color further, turning vibrant shades of orange, red, yellow, and purple. It looks spectacular and ethereal when backlit by the sun, so choose your planting position wisely to make the most of this effect. For wildlife, the redbud doesn't disappoint—its flowers are loved by bees, particularly in its native area, and leafcutter bees use its leaves to line their nests.

ID NOTES

Leaves Heart-shaped, bright red; in fall, deep dark red, orange, yellow, and purple

Twigs Dark brown and speckled

Flowers Pink, pealike, borne in clusters

Seeds Pealike pods with flattened, brown seeds

Bark Red-brown with deep fissures

CARE NOTES

Very little pruning is necessary, apart from the removal of crossing or dead branches (see pp.158–159). Keep the soil moist but not boggy while the tree is establishing. Mulch annually in fall to help retain moisture.

ID NOTES

Leaves Palmate with five-, seven-, or nine-pointed lobes; orange-red, purple, and gold in fall

Twigs Variable, but always bearing opposite buds

Flowers Borne in small, red, hanging clusters

Seeds Paired samara (winged seeds)

Bark Varied

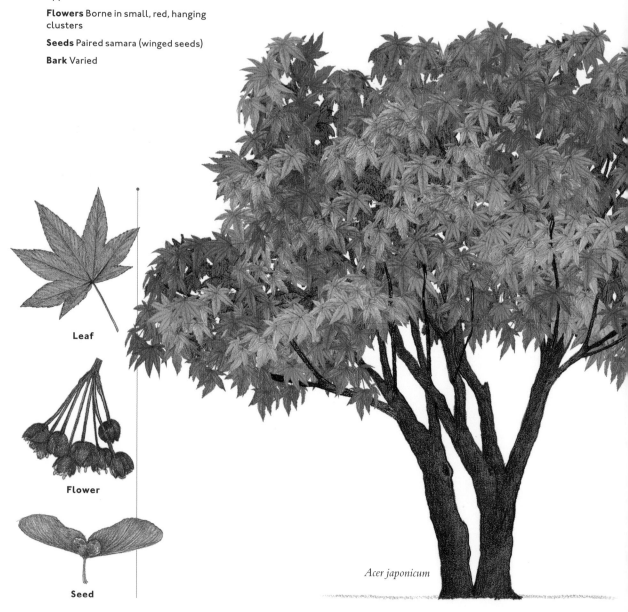

Leaf

Flower

Seed

Acer japonicum

JAPANESE MAPLE

Acer **spp.**

Available in a huge variety of shapes and sizes, Japanese maples are prized for their fantastic fall color; compact, graceful size; and slow-growing habit, making them an excellent choice for small gardens. They also grow well in pots. They require very little pruning and, as long as they're in a sheltered spot away from drying winter winds, they will last for years, providing many seasons of color and interest.

There's a range of Japanese maples to choose from—all have spectacular fall color. Some, such as *Acer palmatum* var. *disssectum*, also have delicate filigree leaves, while others, such as coral bark maples (*A. p.* 'Sango-kaku'), have interesting bark that is a focal point in winter.

Choose your Japanese maple carefully—*A. japonicum* grows as a small tree, while *A. palmatum* is more shrublike, as it grows broader than it does tall. All species are slow-growing, so buy the largest specimen you can afford. Most Japanese maples grow best in shade or partial shade, especially variegated types, which may suffer leaf scorch if they receive too much sun. For sunnier situations, opt for a green-leaved maple that develops red or purple fall leaf color, as it needs some sun for the colorful pigments to develop fully.

Because they're compact and slow-growing, Japanese maples work well in pots. Grow in a good commercial potting mix with added sterilized topsoil and added sharp sand to aid drainage, and keep the potting mix moist but not saturated.

CARE NOTES

Japanese maples need very little care, but you may need to prune to remove crossing or dead branches from time to time (see pp.158–159). Always prune when dormant (in winter) to prevent "bleeding" (losing sap). Mulch annually in spring to retain soil moisture.

Height/spread 33x26ft (10x8m) after 10–20 years

Life expectancy 100 years

Soil type Loam; acid, slightly alkaline, or neutral; well-drained

Native to East Asia

Hardiness Z 4–9, depending on the cultivar

MAIDENHAIR TREE

Ginkgo biloba

A window into an old world, the maidenhair or ginkgo tree dates back 270 million years. Neither a conifer nor a broadleaf tree, it sits on its own in the Ginkgophyta division of the plant kingdom—all of its relatives in this division are extinct. *Ginkgo biloba* can live for up to 3,000 years. It is the National Tree of China, and it's said that there are ginkgoes planted in temples there that are more than 2,500 years old.

Slow-growing and relatively compact, the maidenhair tree is perfect for a small garden. It's hardy and conical but gently spreads with age. The main attraction is the leaves, which are unusual, fan-shaped, and with no visible leaf veins. They often split in the center, forming two lobes, earning its name *biloba*. Its common name refers to the leaves' resemblance to those of the maidenhair fern. They turn a glorious shade of yellow in fall.

Trees are either male or female (dioecious). Female flowers are followed by ball-shaped fruits, said to smell of rancid butter. It's almost impossible to tell male and female ginkgo trees apart until the female tree is in flower, so if you're determined to avoid a female, it's best not to grow a ginkgo at all. It grows in most conditions and makes a fine street tree, as it's extremely pollution tolerant. Grow it in a sunny spot as a focal point of the garden or as part of an ornamental border.

Ginkgoes are prized for their medicinal properties. The leaves contain ginkgolides, which are used in medicines to improve blood circulation to the brain and are said to relieve symptoms of Alzheimer's, tinnitus, and Raynaud syndrome.

CARE NOTES

Ginkgo is incredibly easy to care for. It requires no pruning and is susceptible to no pests or diseases. However, it needs full sun to thrive and will suffer in shade. Mulch annually in fall or spring to retain soil moisture.

Height/spread 33x13ft (10x4m) after 20 years

Life expectancy 3,000 years

Soil type Chalk, clay, loam, sand; acid, alkaline, or neutral; moist but well-drained

Native to China

Hardiness Z 4–9

ID NOTES

Leaves Fan-shaped with a unique structure unknown in any other living plant; yellow in fall

Twigs Red-brown with alternate spurs

Flowers Long yellow catkins (male) and clusters of small flowers on pedicels (female)

Fruit Technically a naked seed, it is round and unpleasant smelling

Bark Gray, furrowed, and corky

Leaf

Fruit

Flower

Trees for autumn colour

SWEET GUM

Liquidambar styraciflua

One of the most beautiful trees you can plant in your garden, sweet gum has magnificent fall color, with leaves turning shades of red, purple, yellow, and orange before falling. Gray, ridged bark adds winter interest. Plant your sweet gum in the sunniest part of your garden for the most dramatic fall color and make sure it's in the perfect spot to see it in its full glory.

With a reasonable growth rate and a conical habit when young (more rounded with age), sweet gum is perfect for smaller gardens, where it makes a striking focal point. Birds and squirrels eat the fruits and may use mature trees for nesting. Being wind-pollinated, the male flowers are packed with pollen and attract bees. The only downside is the hard, spiky seed pods, which can cause injury if you slip or fall on them and are hard to rake up.

Sweet gum takes its name from the sweet, sticky resin that is sometimes exuded from the bark. Historically, this was used in folk medicine and has also been used to make chewing gum. There are several cultivars available, including 'Worplesdon', which has a conical shape; 'Andrew Hewson', which is smaller than the species; and 'Happydaze', which is sterile and so doesn't produce the spiky seed pods. Other cultivars have features such as variegated leaves.

CARE NOTES

Sweet gum is largely free of pests and diseases. Pruning isn't necessary, but remove damaged, crossing, or diseased stems (see pp.158–159). Water well as it becomes established, particularly in prolonged dry spells. Mulch annually, in spring or fall, to retain soil moisture.

Height/spread 33x20ft (10x6m) after 20 years

Life expectancy 150 years

Soil type Clay, loam, sand; acid to slightly alkaline; moist but well-drained

Native to Southeastern US and the cloud forests of Central America

Hardiness Z 5–9

Leaves Maplelike but star-shaped and with deeper lobes; red, orange, yellow, and purple in fall

Twigs Green to yellow-brown, developing gray, corky growths with age; leaf buds often sticky, with greeny-orange, shiny scales

Flowers Male and female catkins appear high up on the same tree in spring; male are red-blushed and form in tight, candlelike clusters; female are spherical and hang individually

Fruit/seed Prickly, spherical seed pods known as "gumballs" develop from female flowers, hanging from the tree into fall

Bark Deeply ridged after about 25 years

Leaf

Female flower

Male flower

Seed pod

Trees for fall color

ID NOTES

Leaves Large, oval, green, glossy; red, orange, and yellow in fall

Twigs Red-brown to gray, with pointed buds, darkening to brown in the winter

Flowers Borne in tiny, green-white clusters

Fruit Blue-purple berries

Bark Dark gray and flaky, developing furrows with age

Leaf

Twig

Flower

TREE PROFILES

BLACK TUPELO

Nyssa sylvatica

This beautiful small tree has glossy, green leaves that turn incredible shades of orange, red, and yellow in fall, rivaling Japanese maple but growing to a more impressive size—though it still works well in a small garden. Its deep purple berries look beautiful against the backdrop of fall leaves, and birds eat them, too.

Black tupelo has a pleasing conical shape, growing symmetrically to just 16x13ft (5x4m) over 20 years or so. It does best in full sun to partial shade. It thrives in a moist, acidic soil and will do particularly well in heavy clay soils. On drier soils, it will need lots of additional watering, so you're better off choosing a Japanese maple (see pp.126–127). There are several cultivars available, including 'Jermyns Flame', which has particularly striking fall color.

For a lesser-known but possibly even more dramatic-looking tree, choose the Chinese tupelo (*Nyssa sinensis*). Smaller than its American cousin, it's ideal for urban gardens and makes a fine street tree, too. Grown as a tree or large shrub, it bears bronze foliage that develops fiery red, orange, and yellow coloring before falling during the season. Its flowers are inconspicuous clusters of green and white, and its berries are fairly unremarkable, too. This tree is grown purely for its foliage, which is as dramatic as it comes. Like the black tupelo, the Chinese tupelo is also better suited to moist soils and can be grown near a pond or stream.

CARE NOTES

Grow in a sheltered spot, away from strong winds. Tupelo trees have a long taproot, which can be damaged when it is transplanted, so it's best to plant them from young, pot-grown plants only. Avoid pruning unless absolutely necessary, and keep well watered in the first couple of years.

Height/spread 26x26ft (8x8m) after 50 years

Life expectancy 70 years

Soil type Loam, sand; acid or neutral; moist but well-drained (tolerates boggy soil for short periods)

Native to North America

Hardiness Z 3–9

STAG'S HORN SUMACH

Rhus typhina

A small tree or shrub, this is dramatic in ornamental borders and container displays alike. It has large, green pinnate leaves that turn glorious shades of red and orange in fall.

Female trees bear beautiful clusters of berries that persist into winter. The berries are eaten by a number of bird species in its native North America. They're edible for us, too. Although *Rhus typhina* isn't one of the *Rhus* species used for making the sumac spice (typically used in Mediterranean cuisine and one of the main ingredients in za'atar), the dried berries can be ground to make a passable substitute. This tree grows well in a container, which also helps deal with its tendency to sucker (see below).

ID NOTES

Leaves Large, pinnate; red and orange in fall

Twigs Stout, reddish-brown, and fuzzy

Flowers Cone-shaped yellow clusters

Fruit/seed Cone-shaped clusters of red berries

Bark Gray-brown and scaly

Flower

Fruit

CARE NOTES

Sumach has a tendency to sucker (send out new shoots from the roots), which can be a problem in small gardens. A pot will contain its suckering tendencies and also produce a smaller tree. You can "containerize" the tree in the ground by placing an impermeable membrane—such as paving slabs—around the roots. Cut off any suckers that appear. Avoid growing it near lawns or boundaries.

Height/spread Up to 26x26ft (8x8m) after 20 years

Life expectancy 50 years

Soil type Loam, sand; acid, alkaline, or neutral; moist but well-drained

Native to North America

Hardiness Z 3–8

Leaf

Seed

Flower

PAPERBARK MAPLE

Acer griseum

One of the most glorious trees
you can grow in a small garden,
the paperbark maple comes into its
own over the fall months, when its
leaves turn fiery shades of
red and orange.

The beautiful papery, peeling bark (which
earns the paperbark its name) steals the
show throughout winter. Choose a spot
for planting where you can see it from
indoors and appreciate its beauty even
when it's too cold to venture outside.

Paperbark maple is a slow-growing
tree and will take 20 years or more to
reach its full size. Its nectar-rich flowers
are attractive to pollinators, which include
birds in its native China.

ID NOTES

Leaves Palmate with three green leaflets;
orange-red in fall

Twigs Slender and brown with light spots
(lenticels) and dark brown, sharply pointed
buds

Flowers Clusters of small, green hanging
flowers

Seeds Paired samara (winged seeds)

Bark Peeling, like paper

CARE NOTES

Grow in a sheltered spot. There should be no
reason to prune, but remove dead or crossing
branches (see pp.158–159) on both young and
older trees when the tree is dormant (winter),
as it can bleed sap if pruned at other times of
year. Mulch in spring to retain soil moisture.

Height/spread 39x26ft (12x8m) after
20 years

Life expectancy 150 years

Soil type Loam, sand; acid, alkaline, or
neutral; moist but well-drained

Native to China

Hardiness Z 4–8

PALM
TREES

Palms are often overlooked as garden trees. While they usually don't absorb as much carbon dioxide as other types of trees (owing to the comparative lack of leaf cover) and are much less attractive to native wildlife, they do still have a role in gardens—whether that's as an evergreen focal point or part of a tropical plant display. Palm trees come in a range of shapes and sizes and many are compact, making them a reliable choice for a small plot. Many are also salt- and wind-tolerant, so they are a good option if you live near the coast. Most palms need tropical or subtropical temperatures to thrive, but some can be grown outdoors in cooler climates; bear in mind that most will grow smaller in our gardens than in their native tropical regions. Hardy palms make excellent structural plants in tropical displays and work well when planted with bananas and bamboos.

CABBAGE PALM

Cordyline australis

The cabbage palm is not a true palm; it's tall and often single trunked, although branching can sometimes occur after flowering.

In summer, the cabbage palm bears masses of fragrant white flowers, beloved by bees, and its berries are eaten by birds. It has large, evergreen rosettes of long, sword-shaped, dark green leaves. One of the easiest exotic trees to grow, it's a good choice for a coastal location and is hardy down to 16°F (-9°C). For small gardens, it will grow happily in a pot, although bear in mind that its height will be restricted in a container—it may reach only 6½ft (2m) tall—and you'll need to repot it from time to time, which can be tricky for large specimens.

ID NOTES

Leaves Sword-shaped, green, borne in clusters

Flowers Cream-white, fragrant panicles

Fruit Clusters of white berries

Bark Corky and gray

Height/spread 26x13ft (8x4m) after 20–50 years

Life expectancy 50–100 years

Soil type Loam, sand, chalk, clay; acid, alkaline, or neutral; moist but well-drained

Native to New Zealand

Hardiness Z 9–11

Bark

Fruit

CARE NOTES

Cabbage palms need little regular pruning but respond well to renovation pruning, whereby you cut the tree right back to the ground in spring to encourage new growth or change its shape. You can also tidy it from time to time, removing old, dead, or straggly leaves. Pot-grown cabbage palms need extra watering and the top few centimeters of the potting mix replaced annually. Those in large pots may never need repotting, but those in smaller containers quickly outgrow them.

CANARY ISLAND DATE PALM

Phoenix canariensis

A large palm tree, the Canary Island date palm has huge, fan-shaped green leaves and clusters of cream-yellow flowers held on long, arching stems.

Despite being native to the Canary Islands, this palm is hardy down to 21°F (-6°C) and grows without problems in a sunny, sheltered spot. In its home range, it can reach 49ft (15m) or more, but in cooler climates, a height of 10–13ft (3–4m) is more realistic. As with many palms, its trunk develops as its old leaves fall off. Canary Island date palms come in a variety of sizes, from 3ft (1m) tall (in 8in/20cm pots) to 10ft (3m), sold in large buckets. It grows slowly, so buy the biggest one you can afford. It will grow well in a large pot.

ID NOTES

Leaves Large, fan-shaped

Flowers Small, off-white, on stalks up to 6½ft (2m) long

Fruit Yellow-orange, on female trees

Bark Fibrous

CARE NOTES

Despite being palm trees, these plants need watering in dry weather—don't let the soil around the palm dry out. If growing in pots, repot every couple of years into a slightly larger pot. When not repotting, top-dress with fresh potting mix in spring. If you need to protect your palm in cold weather, use strong twine to tie all the leaves together to protect the crown.

Bark

Fruit

Height/spread 39x26ft (12x8m) after 20–50 years

Life expectancy 50–150 years

Soil type Loam; acid or neutral; well-drained

Native to Canary Islands

Hardiness Z 9–11

MEDITERRANEAN FAN PALM

Chamaerops humilis

This palm is easy to grow as long as it's planted in a sheltered, sunny spot, although it will tolerate a little shade.

The Mediterranean fan palm is native to southwestern Europe, where it reaches heights of 16ft (5m), with its leaves attaining lengths of 5ft (1.5m). However, it won't grow that big in cooler areas, especially in a container, as it's incredibly slow-growing. New leaves quickly develop to replace old or damaged leaves. It's hardy down to 10°F (-12°C) and is tolerant of salt and wind, making it ideal for coastal gardens.
 While it might not fruit in certain climates, the fruit is eaten by badgers in Spain, which spread the seeds.

ID NOTES

Leaves Large, fan-shaped

Flowers Yellow, in short panicles

Fruit/seed Orange-yellow, in clusters

Bark Fibrous

CARE NOTES

Water well in the first year after planting, and then afterward water only when the rootball starts to dry out. There's usually no need to water in winter. Pruning is not needed, but you may want to remove lower leaves as they turn brown.

Bark

Fruit

Height/spread 8x5ft (2.5x1.5m) after 20–50 years

Life expectancy 50–150 years

Soil type Loam; acid or neutral; well-drained

Native to Mediterranean

Hardiness Z 8–11

CHUSAN PALM

Trachycarpus fortunei

A tall-growing palm tree, the chusan palm has a thick, fibrous trunk and fan-shaped, dark green leaves. It's perfect for growing in exotic and tropical planting schemes and is hardy enough to survive all year round in American gardens in the Pacific Northwest, upper South, and Mid-Atlantic without protection.

Grow the chusan palm in a sunny or shady spot, in the ground or in a pot, but make sure it's sheltered—the leaves can take quite a battering from the wind. As the fibrous trunk grows, it sheds its leaves. The trunk can grow up to 12in (30cm) per year.

These palms are dioecious, meaning they bear either male or female flowers. Male flowers are tiny and yellow but appear in huge clusters, while female flowers are pale yellow and look less dramatic, and these turn into blue-black berries if there's a male tree nearby.

For a neater appearance, you can "strip" the trunk by removing the old, hairy leaves. This does not harm the plant or make it less hardy, but reveals a smooth, pale trunk with a thinner diameter. Using an old bread knife or similar, start at the bottom and use the knife to help you remove individual leaf pieces. It's a time-consuming job, but many think it's worth the finished look.

CARE NOTES

Avoid planting too deeply—ensure that the base of the trunk is visible and remove any soil that piles up around it. Water well until the plant is established. Protect it from wind, as this can damage the leaves and make them look unsightly.

Height/spread 39x10ft (12x3m) after 20–50 years

Life expectancy 50–150 years

Soil type Chalk, loam, sand; acid, alkaline, or neutral; well-drained

Native to Southeast to Central Asia

Hardiness Z 7–11

ID NOTES

Leaves Fan-shaped, dark green, up to 3ft (1m)

Flowers Yellow, borne in arching sprays

Fruit Clusters of blue–black berries

Bark Fibrous

Bark

Fruit

PINDO PALM

Butia capitata

The pindo palm is slow-growing and has blue-green, fan-shaped, feathery leaves that arch from its fibrous trunk.

One of the hardiest feather palms available, it will tolerate temperatures down to 14°F (-10°C). Grow it in a sheltered, sunny spot in well-drained soil. Its other common name, jelly palm, comes from the fact that its fruit is used to make jellies. The natural taste of the fruit is described as a rich pineapple flavor.

Pindo palm is one of the best palms for growing in pots, as its roots respond well to being restricted and it's very slow-growing. Choose a pot slightly larger than the rootball and plant into organically enriched potting mix.

Height/spread 10x10ft (3x3m) after 20–50 years

Life expectancy 80 years

Soil type Loam; acid or neutral; well-drained

Native to South America

Hardiness Z 9–11

Bark

Fruit

ID NOTES

Leaves Fan-shaped and feathery

Flowers Yellow-white, held on long, arching stems

Fruit/seed Yellow-orange fruit

Bark Fibrous

CARE NOTES

Water well until the plant is established and then only to keep the soil moist. Remove old leaves to keep it looking its best. Feed pot-grown plants with a general-purpose fertilizer every couple of weeks in the growing season. Tie the fronds over the crown to protect the tree in winter, or move potted plants indoors.

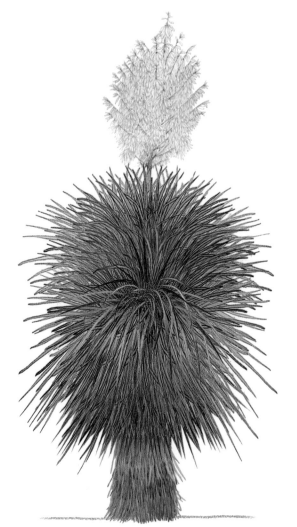

YUCCA

Yucca rostrata

A hardy palm, *Yucca rostrata* can be grown outdoors, as long as it doesn't sit in wet soil.

It's slow-growing and dramatic looking, bearing masses of blue-green, sword-shaped leaves, from which an enormous flower spike appears in summer. Grow in well-drained, alkaline soil in a sheltered, sunny spot. Make sure it can drain freely in winter—add stones to the hole when planting to increase drainage if you need to. You could also grow it in a raised bed or a pot with plenty of drainage. Pot-grown specimens can be brought outside in summer as part of an exotic container display and then taken indoors again in fall if you live in a particularly cold region. *Y. filamentosa* is also hardy and grows as a medium-sized shrub.

These yuccas are not to be confused with *Y. gloriosa*, which may be grown as a houseplant in some areas. *Y. gloriosa* requires tropical warmth, so it is unlikely to survive outdoors even in the mildest of winters.

Height/spread 13x8ft (4x2.5m) after 20–50 years

Life expectancy 50–100 years

Soil type Chalk, loam, sand; alkaline or neutral; well-drained

Native to Central America

Hardiness Z 5–11

Bark

Fruit

ID NOTES

Leaves Blue-green, sword-shaped

Flowers Cream-white on a long stalk

Fruit Oblong, dark blue-brown

Bark Fibrous, comprising old, dead leaves

CARE NOTES

Water sparingly throughout summer and reduce this in fall, stopping completely by October.

PLANT, PRUNE, CARE

*Understanding the basics of planting and caring for your tree
is the key to having it grow successfully. Learn how to plant
bare-root and potted trees, plus essential pruning techniques
and how to spot the early signs of pests and diseases to
ensure your tree will thrive for decades to come.*

Choosing and planting your tree

Once you have chosen which type of tree you want to plant, you need to find a good specimen. Trees are sold in different ways, and your choice may depend on your budget and the time of year you want to plant, as well as finding a good, healthy tree. You'll find a selection of trees at garden centers, but there's often a much greater range at tree nurseries and online.

When shopping for your tree, you will come across "bare-root" and "container-grown" (or "pot-grown") trees. These refer to how the trees are sold and determine how and when you plant them. For additional considerations when buying fruit trees, see pp.150–151.

A bare-root tree
Starting life in open ground, a bare-root tree is dug up when it is dormant in fall and winter and is sold without any soil around it— simply with its "bare roots" exposed. As it's dormant, digging it up doesn't harm it. Look for a good mass of roots that are not broken or growing in a circular shape. It's best to plant your tree right away, but if you can't, then you can "heel it in" by submerging the roots in soil or

sawdust for a few days to stop them from drying out. Plant your tree between late fall and early spring, before it starts growing. A bare-root tree is usually cheaper than a container-grown tree, and you tend to have more varieties to choose from.

A container-grown tree
Grown and sold in a pot, as its name suggests, a container-grown tree has the advantage that it is available to buy all year round and can be planted all year, too (although it's best to avoid summer, when conditions are usually dry). It tends to be more expensive than a bare-root tree, and you may have fewer options to choose from. But it can establish more quickly than a bare-root tree. Make sure the tree looks healthy and is not pot-bound (with roots filling the pot).

What age tree to buy

You can buy a tree at any age, but most are between 1 and 5 years old. Young trees are cheapest and establish more quickly than older trees, which can "sulk" for a couple of years after planting and not grow much. Unless you want a challenge, avoid really young trees, known as saplings, which need formative pruning and aren't robust enough to resist attack from pests such as deer and squirrels. A tree between 2 and 4 years is ideal. Young trees are mostly sold as standard trees, which have a clear stem and distinct head of branches. For guidelines about fruit trees, see pp.150–151.

When to plant a tree

Trees should be planted in soil that's moist but well drained. Frozen, dry, or waterlogged soil should be avoided. Fall is typically the best season to plant a tree, as the soil is still warm from summer, and fall rains keep the soil moist. This should lead to quick establishment of the tree, which should be able to put on root growth before entering winter dormancy, helping it grow better come spring.

Early spring is the next best time to plant a tree, as the soil is starting to warm up and is moist after winter. There's plenty of time for the tree to establish before summer dries the soil, although it's a good idea to continue watering your tree in the first two years, especially during dry periods (see pp.152–153).

Many trees are successfully planted in winter, but avoid planting your tree if the soil is frozen. You can plant a tree in summer, but bear in mind that summer soils tend to be dry, so you will need to water your tree regularly to ensure it establishes well.

Preparing the ground

Before planting your tree, prepare the soil thoroughly. This includes soil over a much larger area than just the planting hole to encourage the roots to spread out well. Dig over the soil and remove any weeds. Avoid adding organic matter, as this will continue to break down after planting and could cause the planting area to "sink," resulting in the tree roots sitting lower in the soil than they should. Add organic matter as a mulch around the planted tree instead (see p.149). If you have very heavy clay or sandy soil, then choose trees that will thrive in these conditions. Clay soil may be easier to manage if a fork is used to break up large clumps.

How to plant a tree

Your planting technique differs only slightly with bare-root and container-grown trees. Soil depth, size and shape of planting hole, and watering requirements are the same regardless of how and when you plant.

1 Soak the roots before planting. For a bare-root tree (see image), remove the wrapping and stand the roots in water for at least 30 minutes before planting. Soak pot-grown trees so the rootball is saturated.

2 Prepare the hole by digging a square hole that's wider but not deeper than your tree's rootball. Square holes help the roots spread via the corners. Lightly fork the base and sides of the hole.

3 Remove the tree from its container for a pot-grown tree (see image). Gently tease out any roots of pot-grown trees that are circling around the inside of the pot. Cut off damaged roots of pot-grown or bare-root trees.

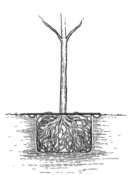

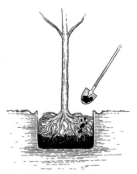

4 Position the tree by standing it in the planting hole, ensuring the top of the rootball, or "soil tide mark" on the stem of bare-root trees, sits level with the soil's surface—lay a cane over the planting hole to help you.

5 Backfill around the rootball with soil, shaking the tree gently to help the soil settle around the roots and watering well as you fill. Firm the soil gently with your heel so that there's good contact between the roots and the soil.

6 If you are staking your tree, choose a sturdy stake. Hammer it into the soil at a 45° angle, taking care to avoid any tree roots. Attach the stake to the tree trunk at one-third of the tree's height using an adjustable tree tie.

Do you need to stake a tree?

Nearly all newly planted trees need staking. This prevents wind rock, which can damage the roots, from reducing the amount of nutrients and water they can absorb and making the tree vulnerable to toppling over.

There are various methods of tree staking. For most trees, a single stake attached to the tree at one-third of its height is sufficient. Ensure the stake is 24in (60cm) into the ground so it doesn't move. Insert the stake on the side of the prevailing wind so the tree isn't blown into the stake.

Preventing animal damage

Depending on where you live and how rural your garden is, you may need to provide protection from animals. Deer and gray squirrels can damage the bark on a new tree, killing it. Rabbits can also eat the bark on young trees, causing problems. Other mammals, such as voles, can nibble at a tree but are unlikely to cause major problems. Using mammal-proof tree guards can prevent the worst damage.

Planting into a pot

Some trees, such as dwarf apples, Japanese maples, and olives, can grow quite well in pots. Choose the largest pot you have room for and use a peat-free, organically enriched potting mix. Add potting mix to about one-third of the pot's depth. Place the tree in the pot to check how it will sit—it needs to be at the same level as it was growing in the ground. When you're happy with the depth, back-fill with more potting mix and water thoroughly. See p.153 for care of a tree in a pot.

Planting a hedge

Hedges can be planted in single or double rows, depending on how big a space you have and how dense you want the hedge to be.

After planting

You may consider adding an organic mulch around the tree after planting and watering. Use garden compost, composted bark or wood chips, or well-rotted animal manure. Simply apply a thick layer around the base of the tree, but not against the trunk. Not only will this preserve water and suppress weeds, it will also slowly feed your newly planted tree, as well as feeding soil microbes such as bacteria and fungi, which in turn aid tree growth. Water the tree well, then keep it watered during dry spells for at least the first year.

Choosing a fruit tree

Fruit trees are available in many shapes and sizes, so it's possible to choose one to suit the space you have, from a large spreading tree to one that grows against a fence or one that thrives in a pot. The size is controlled by the rootstock that the tree is growing on, while the shape can be determined by pruning. A little research before you buy will help you choose the most suitable tree.

Fruit trees are sold at different ages and sizes, depending on how they will be grown. A "whip" is up to 1 year old and about 3ft (1m) tall, with a central stem and few or no branches. A "feathered whip" is older and up to 6½ft (2m) tall, with side branches. A "maiden" is similar to a whip but usually produced by budding or grafting (see Rootstocks). A feathered maiden is older, with six branches. A bush fruit tree is 2 to 3 years old and has been pruned to form a head of several main branches. If growing a fruit tree as a standard, then a 2- to 3-year-old bush tree, where the formative pruning has been already done for you, is ideal. For a trained tree (see opposite), go for a whip or a maiden, as they're easier to prune into the shape you want.

Rootstocks

Some trees are grafted onto the root system of another tree, known as a rootstock. This controls the growth and vigor of the tree so that it grows smaller (or sometimes more strongly) than it would on its own roots. This is useful when training a tree into a particular shape where less vigorous growth is needed. A rootstock can also improve disease resistance and control when and how much a tree fruits. Some are best for trees in pots. Often used for fruit trees, rootstocks are also used for some ornamentals.

Rootstocks have names such as "dwarfing" and "semidwarfing" and a code (for example, there are M or MM rootstocks). Other rootstocks include Quince, Gisela, and Colt. One of the most popular is MM106 (semidwarfing), used for apple trees.

PLANT, PRUNE, CARE

Some guidance is given on rootstocks in the fruit tree profiles (see pp.64–77).

Pollination

Most fruit trees are pollinated by insects, such as bees. Some, including apples and pears, need a "pollination partner" for the most successful fruit development. A pollination partner is simply another tree of the same genus that flowers at the same time to enable cross-pollination to occur. Check these needs when buying your fruit tree; a specialist nursery will be able to offer reliable advice.

Untrained fruit trees

A standard is a typical-shaped fruit tree with a bare trunk and branches and is over 6½ft (2m). A specimen up to 13ft (4m) tall gives instant impact but will grow very slowly. A standard is best grown on M9 for a small apple or MM111 or M25 for larger trees, Quince A for pears, Colt for a cherry or plum, and St. Julien A for a peach.

Trained fruit trees

Fan and espalier These attractive trees are trained flat into a fan shape or, for an espalier, with horizontal branches. Train them up a fence or wall or along wires to mark a boundary. Growing the tree against a vertical surface, with its branches exposed, allows the sun to reach and ripen the fruits more easily. A fan or espalier needs to be pruned annually (see pp.160–161). It is best grown on a dwarfing or semidwarfing rootstock, such as MM106 or M9 for apples, the semivigorous St. Julien A for plums, Gisela 5 and Colt for cherries, Quince A for pears, and Torinel for peaches.

Stepover tree This is the smallest fruit tree and is low growing, ideal for edging borders and paths. It is best grown on M27 for apples, Pixy for plums, and Quince C for pears.

Cordon tree This is a small tree usually planted in a row to make a fruiting hedge. It is grown on a single stem with short side branches and needs to be planted 2½-3ft (0.75–1m) from others in the row and tied to supporting wires. It is best grown on a dwarfing rootstock, such as M9 for apples, Pixy for plums, and Quince C for pears.

Supporting your trained tree

By training your tree, you are committing to regularly pruning it to maintain its shape (see pp.160–161). Support is key, too: even those grown against a wall or fence will need tying into supports (such as wires or bamboo canes) for the first few years.

Caring for your tree

Ultimately, a tree doesn't need much care, but in the first couple of years, you will need to keep a close eye out to ensure your garden tree is growing well. A pot-grown tree will need extra care in the form of watering, feeding, and top-dressing—but all newly planted trees need watering when conditions are dry. Checking the stake every now and then is important, too.

Just like any plant you add to your garden, you want your tree to do well. So check on it regularly, assess what it needs, and then provide it. Your tree will grow beautifully.

Watering a tree in the ground

Mature trees have extensive root systems, aided by fungi, that enable them to draw up water from the soil. The root systems of most trees are as wide as their canopy, but some also have deep taproots that extend far below the soil's surface, where they can literally "tap" into a water source usually unavailable to other plants.

A newly planted tree won't have an established root system to rely on yet, so it will need some help from you. It's a good idea to water your tree every few weeks for up to two years after planting. This will help it become established and develop a good root system. Don't overthink the process—water weekly in the first six months (more if you're on sandy soil or conditions are particularly dry and sunny), ensuring the soil around the tree is completely soaked with each application; use one to two whole watering cans of water. Reduce this to every couple of weeks to a month as the tree grows, and be mindful of the seasons—don't water at all in winter, and check before watering in early spring, when the soil is often cold and wet.

Bear in mind that it's possible to overwater your tree, which will then produce roots close to the surface of the soil, making it more vulnerable to drought and more likely to topple in high winds. Check the soil if you think you may be watering too much.

PLANT, PRUNE, CARE

Using a trowel, dig down to a depth of 2in (5cm). If the soil is dry and dusty, water. If it's damp, hold off watering for another week.

Feeding
Most trees don't need regular feeding, but an annual mulch of well-rotted manure or garden compost provides a slow-release nutrient boost for your garden tree. For the best results, water before applying the mulch, as the mulch will then conserve moisture, as well as feeding the soil.

Weeding
Keep an area 3ft (1m) in diameter around your tree free from weeds, as these can quickly grow and smother your tree—especially if it's a sapling—and compete with the tree for water and nutrients. Weeds such as bindweed can engulf a young tree, causing growth to become distorted. Some rootstocks (usually those for espalier, stepover, and pot-grown fruit trees, such as M27 and M9 for apples, Quince C and Quince Eline for pears, Pixy for plums, and Gisela for cherries) need weed- and grass-free soil to grow well. For these, you may need to ensure bare soil around your tree trunk for its whole life, or mulch regularly to suppress weed growth.

Checking the stake
Newly planted trees are staked to prevent "wind rock," where wind moves the tree from side to side, tearing new roots and preventing the tree from establishing well. It can take two years for a tree to anchor itself into the soil. It's worth keeping an eye on your tree stake, as it can become loose and stop supporting the tree. Also bear in mind that you will need to loosen your tree tie as the tree grows to prevent rubbing injury to the trunk. If you're using a tree guard, check it to ensure it's not cutting into the tree or hasn't come loose and dispose of it responsibly when it's no longer needed.

Caring for a tree in a pot
Some trees can grow well in pots, but bear in mind that their roots are exposed to a finite amount of soil, water, and nutrients, along with fungi, bacteria, and microbes that aid tree growth. This means you will have to water more often, even if it rains. To keep the soil fresh and replenish some nutrients, each spring, scrape off the top layer and replace with a top-dressing of fresh, enriched potting mix. Add a dose of liquid feed every two weeks in spring and summer as well, especially for fruit trees.

Planting around your tree

You may be content with planting just the tree in your garden, leaving it as the main focal point, and having nothing growing around it. That's fine, but as an alternative, you can plant shrubs and herbaceous plants around the tree to create a beautiful border, which not only adds interest but also provides additional habitats for wildlife, absorbs more carbon, and helps prevent flooding.

Two options for your tree are to make it part of a sunny or shady (woodland) border, where it will work with the shrubs and perennials to create a look and habitat that changes through the seasons. Choose carefully and the shrubs and perennials will flower and/or fruit at different times of year from the tree, creating a longer season of interest.

If your tree is deciduous, grow an evergreen shrub nearby that will draw attention in winter from the tree's bare branches to something more lush and "alive." If your tree flowers in spring, choose perennials that flower in summer. If your tree has bold fall colors, choose plants with a plainer overall look at this time of year that will act as the perfect foil for your end-of-season display—or complementary colors

that will enhance the tree's fall hues. Plants work together above and below ground, sharing nutrients and information, but with a little input from you, they can be put together to make something special. You can add bird and bee boxes to enhance the wildlife appeal (see p.162).

Bear in mind that your tree will absorb a fair amount of water and the soil will therefore be drier here than in other parts of the garden. Also the tree's canopy will cast some shade beneath it. Even in a sunny border, you will need some shade-tolerant plants and plants that can cope with drier than average soil conditions.

Plants for a woodland border

A cool, shady area makes the perfect spot for a woodland border. Trees that would work in a woodland border include birch (see pp.108–109), hawthorn (see pp.84–85), Japanese maple (see pp.126–127), serviceberry (see p.55), tree ferns (see p.59), and dogwoods (see pp.90–91).

Under these, you can plant shade-tolerant shrubs such as guelder rose (*Viburnum opulus*), spindle (see p.101), and holly (see pp.80–81); herbaceous plants such as Solomon's seal (*Polygonatum* × *hybridum*), false goats' beard (*Astilbe*), campions (*Silene*), foxgloves (*Digitalis*), ferns, and hostas; and low perennials such as hellebores, primroses (*Primula*), wood anemones (*Anemone nemorosa*), and sweet woodruff (*Galium odoratum*). In spring, add bulbous plants such as snowflakes (*Leucojum*) and snake's head fritillary (*Fritillaria meleagris*), while fall-flowering Japanese anemones (*Anemone hupehensis*) will tolerate dappled shade.

Plants for a sunny border

There's a huge range of plants for growing in sun and dappled shade. Trees for a sunny border are crab apple (see pp.56–57), most fruit trees, olive (see pp.60–61), strawberry tree (see pp.98–99), crape myrtle (see p.87), and paperbark maple (see p.135). For a more exotic look, a palm could be an option here, too (see pp.136–143).

Shrubs include buddleia, weigela, and rock rose (*Cistus*), while herbaceous plants include catmint (*Nepeta*), lavender (*Lavandula*) and other Mediterranean herbs, ornamental poppies (*Papaver*), agapanthus, bellflowers (*Campanula*), and annuals such as sunflowers (*Helianthus*).

Add vibrant colors against a lush green backdrop and you'll be in good shape. Plan to have something in flower from spring to fall for a lively display and the most wildlife value. Add ornamental grasses such as *Stipa* and *Miscanthus* for structure and a longer season of interest. The best spring bulbs for bees are crocus and alliums, while viper's bugloss (*Echium*) attracts a wide range of pollinators. *Verbena bonariensis*, heleniums, and rudbeckias will provide a late source of nectar and pollen.

How to plant your border

It can be difficult to get plants to establish immediately around trees, as light and soil moisture levels will be lower, but planting 3–6½ft (1–2m) from the trunk should be fine. Plants usually establish better on the sunny side of a tree's trunk. Plant in fall for the best results, paying attention to planting depths and aspect requirements on the plants' labels.

Pruning
your tree

Many trees need some pruning at some stage of their life, but you may be surprised to learn that—with the exception of fruit trees—most can be left alone, with minimal pruning. However, a quick prune once a year can keep your tree healthy and maintain a good shape. This can be a good opportunity to check your tree for signs of pests and disease, which can prevent problems in the long term.

Most routine pruning involves using techniques to limit the size of the tree; improve its shape; or, in the case of fruit trees, encourage more flowering (and therefore fruiting) spurs to form (see pp.160–161). Pruning to remove crossing, dead, or damaged stems is also worthwhile and can prolong the health of your tree. In some (thankfully rare) cases, you may need to prune out infection, such as canker (see p.166) or silver leaf disease (see p.167).

When to prune
Deciduous trees are usually pruned in winter, as it's easier to see what you're doing to the branches and to assess the overall shape. Exceptions include tender deciduous trees, which are best pruned in late spring, and stone fruit trees (including cherries, apricots, peaches, plums, and nectarines), which are best pruned in summer to prevent infection from the diseases silver leaf and bacterial canker. Some trees, such as walnut (*Juglans regia*) and mulberry (see p.77), bleed heavily (ooze sap from the pruning wound), so they need to be pruned at certain times of year to avoid long-term damage.

While less likely to need pruning, evergreen trees should be pruned in spring, before growth starts, apart from pine trees, which need to be pruned in summer.

Preparing to prune
Check beforehand that the tree is on your property.

For safety, always check the tree before starting—especially older trees. Thick gloves, goggles, and a hard hat are necessary for working on mature trees, when branches could fall on you or you could get sawdust in your eyes. Young trees have fewer, if any, such risks. If you're in any doubt, employ a professional tree surgeon to do the work for you.

Always use the sharpest pruning shears, loppers, and pruning saw, as these will ensure the cleanest cuts. If handling diseased material, clean your tools with antibacterial and antifungal solution to prevent the tools from spreading the infection from the material to other parts of the tree.

Pruning a deciduous tree

When you plant a tree, you may need to carry out some formative pruning to encourage the development of a good initial shape. Many nursery-grown trees will already have had some formative pruning, which you'll simply need to keep up.

However, if you grow a tree from a very young whip, you'll need to prune it yourself to help the tree develop a good shape, with a clear trunk and well-branched canopy. Remove sideshoots from the bottom third of the tree to ensure a strong central trunk, then cut by half all of the sideshoots in the middle of the stem.

How to make a pruning cut

Make each cut carefully to reduce the risk of infection and keep the tree growing into a shape you want.

Cutting to a bud
Make a clean cut just above a bud. Angle the cut away from the bud so moisture doesn't pool on the wound. Don't leave too much stem above the bud, as this will die back, attracting disease.

Cutting back to the stem or trunk
When removing a young shoot, cut it back flush with the stem using a clean cut so that the bark heals well.

Leave those at the top unpruned to form the initial branch framework.

For the basic methods and principles of regular pruning, see opposite. For detailed advice on pruning specific trees, consult a tree pruning book or visit rhs.co.uk/advice/plant-care/pruning.

Pruning a mature tree

You may inherit an old tree that needs a prune to reshape it or reduce its size. This is usually done to thin the canopy to allow in sunlight (especially for fruit trees), to raise the canopy to enable people or cars to move beneath it, or to reduce the tree's height. Bear in mind that bad pruning can make a mature tree unstable or look unsightly, and you may be best off getting in the professionals.

Pruning an evergreen tree

Evergreens only need minimal pruning: removing dead, diseased, or broken branches, taking care to follow the general shape of the tree. Prune just before new growth starts in spring, using pruning shears to tackle one branch at a time. The exception to this rule is pine trees, which should be pruned during active growth so new buds will develop in time for the following year.

Shears can be used for some trees, but this creates a uniform, formal look that's best for evergreens. If creating a formal shape with shears, wait until late spring so growth has started, which will help cuts heal quickly. Most conifer trees grow on new wood only, so they should be pruned back to new (pliable) growth. Pruning back into old, brown wood will result in unsightly brown patches that never grow back.

Pruning a palm

Palm trees are fairly low maintenance and don't need pruning, but you might want to tidy up brown fronds from time to time. You can do this from late spring to summer, removing hanging, dead, or otherwise unhealthy-looking fronds. Avoid removing green fronds, especially new ones, as this can stress the tree.

Pruning a hedge

Hedges will need a regular trim, up to twice a year for formal hedges but ideally every other year for wildlife hedges, to avoid pruning out the eggs of some moth species. Remember that it's illegal to disturb bird nests,

General pruning

While most ornamental trees need very little pruning, some (especially fruit trees) may need pruning annually to keep them in good shape. Before starting, work out what you want to achieve. Aim for an open shape so that light and air can reach all the branches.

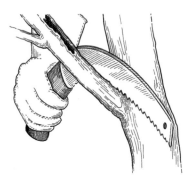

Damaged branch
Remove any damaged branches, cutting just above the branch collar—the swollen area at the base of the branch, from where a scar can form more easily, aiding healing.

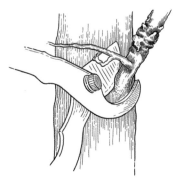

Diseased branch
Cut diseased branches to the trunk, again making sure that you don't cut into the branch collar. Check that you are cutting back to healthy wood.

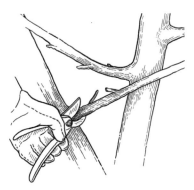

Crossing branches
Remove any branches that are crossing and could rub together, causing wounds, which can weaken the tree, making it more susceptible to diseases.

Removing suckers
Pull suckers from the tree base by hand or cut them to the ground with pruning shears. Suckers from a grafted rootstock may be a different species to your tree.

so you must check your hedge thoroughly before trimming.

For yew hedges, initially shorten side branches only to encourage a more dense growth habit. Wait until the hedge has reached the desired height before cutting the growing tips, as trimming the growing tips can pause growth for a year or two, making it very slow to establish.

Pruning a freestanding fruit tree

Fruit trees should ideally be pruned each year to keep them healthy and producing a larger crop. Unpruned fruit trees grow less productive over time and can become congested.

Apple and pear trees Prune freestanding apples and pears when they're dormant in winter, after the leaves have fallen and before the buds burst. Aim to create an open, goblet or bowl shape with four to five main branches. Shorten the previous season's growth by a third, cutting back to an outward-facing bud so the tree retains an open form. Apples and pears are pruned according to where

Identifying fruiting buds

Like ornamental trees, fruit trees need to be pruned to remove dead, diseased, or crossing branches. But they should also be pruned to maximize productivity. Learn to identify fruiting buds so that you can tailor your pruning to the type of tree you have.

Spur bearers bear fruit buds on wood older than 2 years, and as spurs, which can be identified as knobby buds growing more closely together than the smaller leaf buds.

Tip bearers have their fruit buds at the tips of 1-year-old shoots. They have a more untidy appearance than spur bearers. Partial tip bearers fruit on the tips and some spurs.

PLANT, PRUNE, CARE

their fruit buds form; as their name suggests, these are the buds that will form blossom and then fruits. Fruit trees are separated into three types: spur bearers, partial tip bearers, and tip bearers (see Identifying fruiting buds, opposite). Most apple and pear cultivars bought today are spur bearing, but be aware of how your tree fruits so you can prune it to maximize fruiting potential.

On spur bearers, make sure that fruiting spurs are evenly spaced. If they are congested, thin them to 4–6in (10–15cm) apart. The result will be a balanced tree with plenty of light to ripen the fruits and space for air to circulate, discouraging disease.

On tip bearers and partial tip bearers, be aware that any pruning that involves shortening shoot tips will reduce the yield. Leave branches less than around 8in (20cm) long and shorten longer ones to around four or five buds—as well as bearing fruit from those four or five buds, these cut stems will develop new shoots that will bear fruit the following year.

Plums and cherries Free-standing plums and cherries don't require as much pruning as apples and pears but still benefit from formative pruning and then the thinning of old wood. Plums and other stone fruits such as cherries and apricots are pruned in early spring or midsummer to avoid infection by silver leaf disease.

Trees less than 3 years old should be pruned in late spring, when the buds are bursting or when the tree is just beginning to flower. Shorten stems by around a third and remove damaged, diseased, and crossing branches, aiming for an open goblet shape to maximize airflow and ensure the sun reaches the fruit.

Pruning a trained fruit tree

Fruit trees grown as espaliers, fans, and cordons need to be pruned in summer and winter to maintain a good shape and keep them fruiting well. Summer pruning from August usually involves removing new growth beyond the ripening fruit. Exact pruning techniques and timings differ, depending on the age of your tree. For example, young trees (up to 3 years old) often need specific formative pruning to ensure they grow well.

Always check the RHS pruning advice before carrying out any pruning work on trained fruit trees to ensure you're working at the right time of year for the type of tree you're pruning and that you're pruning out the correct material.

Making the most of trees

Whether it's the tree in your garden or trees in the local community, you can make the most of them in ways that bring benefits to the local community and wildlife and to you and others. Once you've planted your tree, you might notice and get to know other trees in your area. If you're involved in community groups, there will be a whole network of trees out there to explore.

Activities centered around your tree can range from simply feeding the birds to nature walks and organized annual events.

Attracting more birds

Hang feeders from strong branches, attaching a tray beneath the feeder so seed doesn't spill onto the ground (which can attract rats). Choose high-quality seed mixes and straight seeds, such as sunflower seed, with suet and peanuts added to the mix in winter. Clean the feeder regularly to prevent birds from spreading diseases and refill it when needed—never let the food get moldy.

Local trees can also be used to hang bird feeders. Check with your local community group to ensure that this is agreeable. If you're hanging a feeder on a community tree, you may be able to ask others to chip in with the cost of bird seed and maintenance.

Nest boxes can be used to provide homes for birds before the tree develops natural nesting holes. Don't nail the box to the tree, but use wire to fix it around the trunk instead— check the wire annually to make sure it's not cutting into the tree bark.

Making leaf mold

In nature, leaves fall to the ground and break down, gradually returning nutrients to the tree. By gathering leaves, rotting them down, and then using them as a mulch in the form of leaf mold, you can mimic this natural process. Leaf mold is a fantastic resource. Essentially decomposed leaf material aided by fungi rather than bacteria (as in

PLANT, PRUNE, CARE

conventional composting), it contains soil conditioners and trace elements that help your garden grow better. It has many uses—for example, as a mulch around the garden and allotment and as an ingredient in homemade potting mix.

To get the best results, you simply pile leaves together, either in a bespoke bin or cage or in a plastic bag with a few small holes for ventilation (old mulch bags work well) for between one and three years. Then distribute the resulting leaf mold around the garden.

The leaves of all deciduous trees make good leaf mold but break down at different rates. Thin, matte leaves such as birch, hazel, ash, and elm break down in less than 12 months, while waxy leaves such as oak and plane take up to three years. Evergreen leaves and conifer needles take much longer and benefit from being chopped up first.

If you're a member of your local "Friends of" park group, you can suggest leaf-gathering days where leaves from park trees are raked up and stored. Keep them for one year to use as a mulch around the park or up to three to use in potting mixes.

Community activities

Use your community trees as part of a local nature trail, with signs in and around the trees to identify birds and other wildlife that might visit them. You may be able to get permission to let grass grow long around the trees, creating small pockets of meadow to enhance biodiversity. You could organize tree-centered Easter egg hunts and ID and drawing events for children. If there is a local mini-orchard, you could have harvesting and pruning days. Take your neighbors out on bird walks— you'll be amazed how much local wildlife uses the trees you planted.

Resources

For help identifying local trees and engaging with your community of trees, download a tree ID app on your phone or buy a simple tree book. (You may find the tree ID guide listed on p.169 helpful.) Once you've learned your trees, then focus on the birds and other species that use them. There's a whole world out there to explore and get to know—start in your garden or local park, and you never know where your new knowledge might take you.

Troubleshooting

Pests and diseases are a common problem for growers of fruit trees and some deciduous trees, with climate change bringing new challenges. Both pests and diseases are a part of life, and many trees can live with them (although perhaps not with as much vigor as they would otherwise). But in both cases, you may sometimes have to help your tree deal with a problem.

In this section, I will mention some pests and diseases that are particularly widespread or harmful so that you can recognize them if they affect your tree.

Pests and diseases in the garden

In gardening circles, "pest" is used to describe anything from slugs and snails to sawfly, aphids, ants and thrips, moth caterpillars, and leaf-mining fly larvae that are perceived to damage plants. Most of these are not only part of the ecosystem but part of the food chain and are essential for the survival of other species, such as birds. With the exception of slugs and snails, the "damage" caused by them is usually minimal—there's no need to control them on garden trees. However, sometimes, and usually when growing in a compromised ecosystem with few predators such as birds and wasps, these "pests" can multiply faster than usual. A pest, in my view, is only such when present in sufficient numbers to do actual harm. As an apple grower, I know some of my fruit will have codling moth tunnels in them, so I cut my apples before I eat them and eat around the tunnels. That's how I manage the "pest."

That said, there's an increasing number of non-native insects that have found their way to the US and have no natural predators to keep their numbers in check. A few arrived of their own accord, but most were accidentally imported on timber or live plants from other countries. Species from warmer climates can't usually survive our winters, but with climate change, some are managing to and more will do so in future.

Mammals and birds are also sometimes regarded as pests. Deer, squirrels, and rabbits can damage bark, which can kill young trees. These are best dealt with by using a tree guard (see p.149). Birds are considered pests for eating fruit crops such as cherries. Some gardeners net their cherry trees, but I'd rather share my crop with them—there's usually enough for us all.

Many trees can live with a level of infections. However, several new diseases have arrived in recent years, again usually due to importing plants and timber, which are having devastating consequences. There are many more diseases that could hit our shores in the coming years and that experts are keeping an eye on. In the following pages, I've described some of the more common pests and diseases, grouped by the part of the tree most likely to be affected.

Pests and diseases that affect leaves and twigs

Aphids There are many species of aphid, which suck sap from trees and other plants. Most do little harm to the tree and are eaten by a number of birds, including vesper sparrows.

Tree aphids suck plant sap and excrete a sugary substance called honeydew. Honeydew can attract black mold, which coats the leaves and can inhibit photosynthesis, weakening the tree. Woolly aphids are noticeable, as they hide in white, waxy fluff. They're found on ornamental apple trees, cotoneaster, and pyracantha shrubs. Affected stems sometimes develop swellings along the bark, which can burst in winter, creating wounds that expose the tree to fungal infections.

Box moth (*Cydalima perspectalis*) Native to East Asia, box moth was possibly transferred from Canada to the US. The caterpillars eat box and cause severe defoliation. This pest is why you won't find box listed in the tree profile pages.

Horse chestnut leaf miner (*Cameraria ohridella*) This moth, potentially found on six *Aesculus* species in the US, lays eggs on horse chestnut leaves. The larvae bore into the leaves, causing them to drop. In large numbers, and over several years, they can weaken trees.

Oak processionary moth (*Thaumetopoea processionea*) Native to southern Europe, oak processionary moth feeds exclusively on oak trees. Caterpillars form large, arrow-shaped groups on oak tree trunks and can sometimes be seen moving between oak trees. They form large nests on oak trunks and large branches. The caterpillars are covered in small white hairs, which can cause breathing difficulties in humans.

Canker (*Pseudomonas syringae*) Bacterial canker is a common disease of the stems and leaves of *Prunus*, especially plums and cherries, but also apricots and peaches. It causes sunken patches of dead bark, which oozes gum, and small holes in leaves, called "shothole." Trees can live with canker for years without dying, but severe cases can kill the tree. Using the cleanest and sharpest tools, you can literally cut the canker out of the branch. Prune back to around 4–6in (10-15cm) from the affected area into healthy wood. Clean tools using disinfectant afterward to avoid spreading the infection.

Pests and diseases that affect fruits

Apple codling moth (*Cydia pomonella*) This small moth has caterpillars that bore into apples and pears in summer. The exit hole is usually visible, but the damage is most obvious when the fruit is cut open, and you can see the tunnel.

Brown rot (*Monilinia laxa, M. fructigena*) This fungal disease affects apples, pears, plums, cherries, and some ornamental trees, causing brown, rotting patches on the fruit. As the fruits ripen, they develop rotting brown patches, often with white pustules. The best way to control the fungus is to stop it from overwintering. Remove all infected fruit in fall and either put it in the trash or bury it more than 3ft (1m) below ground.

Diseases that affect the whole tree

Honey fungus (*Armillaria* spp.) This attacks and kills the roots of woody and perennial plants, including trees. It's fairly common and is the worst fungal disease in gardens, although some species are less aggressive than others and may not kill their host. The most obvious symptom is white fungal growth between the bark and wood, while clumps of light brown toadstools may appear in fall. Black, shoelacelike strands called rhizomorphs may be found in the trunks of felled trees. It's not possible to control honey fungus; the only way to get rid of it is to dig up and destroy affected plants with as much of the root as possible.

Silver leaf (*Chondrostereum purpureum*) Silver leaf is a fungal disease that affects the wood and leaves of some trees, notably apples, apricots, cherries, plums, hawthorn, poplar, and laburnum. The fungus usually penetrates the wood through pruning wounds. Leaves develop a silvery sheen before the whole branch dies. Older, dead branches may display bracket-shaped fruiting bodies in summer, whitish on top and purple-brown below. When cut, the wood is stained. Infectious spores are most prevalent in winter, so susceptible trees should be pruned in summer. To control silver leaf, remove the affected branch as soon as possible, cutting it back to 4–6in (10–15cm) beyond any stained internal wood. Disinfect all tools afterward and burn or dispose of the infected wood, as it can still fruit when cut and release spores that can reinfect your tree. Don't confuse silver leaf with false silver leaf, which causes silvery leaves, usually due to cold, drought, or other stress. Unlike true silver leaf, which affects one branch at a time, the whole tree is affected and the wood is not stained.

Dutch elm disease (*Ophiostoma ulmi*) This fungal disease, spread by elm bark beetles, was first identified in the US in 1930. Most vulnerable to the disease is the American elm (*Ulmus americana*). Hybrid elms and insecticide have helped control, but not eliminate, the disease.

Ash dieback (*Hymenoscyphus fraxineus*) Accidentally imported from Europe in 2012, but originating in Asia, ash dieback infects trees via airborne spores that penetrate the tree's leaves and then grow inside the tree. Eventually, it blocks the xylem tissues, which transport water around the tree, resulting in its death. There is no remedy.

Fusarium wilt (*Fusarium oxysporum*) This fungal disease affects palm trees, including Canary Island date palm. Symptoms include browning of the fronds and dieback of the frond tips, starting at the base of the plant. Palms can be infected for years before symptoms develop, but the tree usually dies. Like other wilt diseases, including Verticillium wilt, Fusarium is soil borne and is often spread in nurseries. It can also be spread by pruning, so sterilize pruning tools after each use.

Supporting tree-planting projects

Beyond your community, you may want to support tree-planting projects to help get more trees in the ground. Bear in mind, however, that tree planting projects can be hugely problematic, so do your research. Here, I cover some of the pitfalls and recommend a few valuable organizations.

Some organizations are better than others—for example, you may not realize you're donating money to plant trees on rented land, with nothing to guarantee the trees will remain after the land's lease is up. Or, in some countries, that the trees are to be planted on land important to indigenous communities, many of which were not considered or consulted. The Great Green Wall project (see p.24) is only now involving local communities, some 15 years after its inception and after millions of the planted trees died.

And will you ever know if the trees you fund are planted in a way that contributes to the local environment, or if lots of the same tree are planted in straight rows, which have little if any options for wildlife? And will they be cared for so that they absorb carbon dioxide, or left to die so they release it back into the atmosphere?

THE NATURE CONSERVANCY

nature.org/en-us/get-involved/how-to-help/plant-a-billion/
The Nature Conservancy's Plant a Billion Trees campaign is a major forest restoration program. Its goal is to plant a billion trees across the planet to slow the connected crises of climate change and biodiversity loss.

TREE CITY USA

arborday.org/programs/treecityusa/
The Tree City USA program provides communities with a four-step framework to maintain and grow their tree cover. Some 750,000 trees were planted via this program in 2020.

AMERICAN FOREST FOUNDATION

forestfoundation.org
The American Forest Foundation works with a broad coalition of partners across the United States in developing and implementing innovative solutions that engage family forest owners in effectively addressing our nation's most pressing conservation challenges.

Resources

RHS PRUNING INFORMATION

rhs.org.uk/pruning
Information on pruning a range of trees and tree types, with tips on time of year, hygiene, and maximizing fruiting potential.

AMERICAN FORESTS

americanforests.org
A conservation-oriented magazine that has been published since 1895.

THE HIDDEN LIFE OF TREES

Peter Wohlleben, HarperCollins, 2015
How trees communicate, including the importance of fungal networks.

THE OVERSTORY

Richard Powers, Vintage, 2018
A fantastic novel about nine Americans who come together to address the destruction of the forests.

WHAT'S THAT TREE?

DK, 2013
Simple tree identification handbook.

WOODLANDS

Oliver Rackham, HarperCollins, 2012
One of the most significant voices on trees and woodlands in recent history, Oliver Rackham here documents the significance of trees and woodlands over time.

FRIENDS OF THE EARTH INTERNATIONAL FOREST PROGRAM

foe.org/issues/forests/
How Friends of the Earth works to address the root causes of forest destruction and the marginalization of forest-dwelling communities.

GREENPEACE: PROTECT OUR FORESTS

greenpeace.org.uk/wp-content/uploads/2020/07/GP-11-14-Forests-Final.pdf
Information on protecting forests from international environment trust dedicated to the conservation of forests and other ecosystems.

INTERNATIONAL TREE FOUNDATION

internationaltreefoundation.org
International charity for tree planting and conservation across the globe.

RAINFOREST ALLIANCE

rainforest-alliance.org
Charity dedicated to protecting rainforests across the globe.

REWILDING INSTITUTE

rewilding.org
Develops and promotes continental-scale conservation in North America.

SOURCES FOR INFORMATION

p.6 In 2021, more than 400 weather stations broke their heat records:
www.theguardian.com/world/2022/jan/07/heat-records-broken-all-around-the-world-in-2021-says-climatologist

p.6 The Amazon rainforest is thought to emit more carbon dioxide than it can absorb:
www.sciencefocus.com/news/the-amazon-rainforest-now-emits-more-carbon-than-it-absorbs/

p.25 Half of Britain's new forests have been planted not by humans, but by jays:
www.theguardian.com/environment/2021/jun/16/half-the-trees-in-two-new-english-woodlands-planted-by-jays-study-finds

p.26 More than 50 percent of people live in cities now, with nearly 70 percent of the world's human population expected to live in cities by 2050:
www.un.org/development/desa/en/news/population/2018-revision-of-world-urbanization-prospects.html

p.26 A 2019 study predicts a 4°F (2°C) global rise by 2050 will see city temperatures rise exponentially higher:
www.bbc.co.uk/news/newsbeat-48947573

p.29 Some studies have also shown that street trees absorb less carbon dioxide than those growing in more natural environments:
www.frontiersin.org/articles/10.3389/fevo.2016.00053/full

Glossary

BLEEDING
The oozing of sap from a pruning cut after pruning.

BRACT
A modified, often flowerlike leaf, usually growing around the flower.

BRANCH
A large, mature, woody stem.

BUD
A leaf or flower that has not yet opened.

CANOPY
The branches and foliage of a tree.

CARR
A wet woodland where trees adapted to wet soils, such as silver birch and alder, grow.

CATKIN
An elongated cluster of flowers, resembling a lamb's tail, with scaly bracts and typically no petals.

CONE
Usually found on pine trees, botanically it is a mass of scales or bracts and contains the reproductive organs.

DETRITIVORE
Invertebrate, such as an earthworm, that eats and recycles soil detritus.

DORMANCY/DORMANT
A stage of nongrowth, typically in winter but occasionally in high summer.

DOUBLE FLOWER
A flower bred to have extra petals, often so many that you can't see the central part of the flower, where pollen and nectar is formed.

DRUPE
A fleshy fruit containing a single seed, such as cherry, peach, or olive.

FLORET
A small flower, usually making up part of a head of flowers.

FRUITING SPUR
The fruiting buds of a tree, borne on small stems of wood.

HESPERIDIUM
A fruit with sections of pulp inside a rind, such as an orange or lemon.

INFLORESCENCE
A cluster of flowers.

LANCEOLATE
Used to describe leaves shaped like a lance, tapering from a rounded base.

LEADER
The central stem (or trunk) of a tree.

NODE
The point on a stem from which a flower, leaf, or twig will grow.

PALMATE
Used to describe leaves shaped like a hand, having four or more lobes from a single point.

PANICLE
A multibranched cluster of flowers.

PEDICEL
A small stalk, usually carrying a fruit.

PINNATE
Used to describe leaves having a central stem with leaves growing on either side.

RIB
One of the main veins of a leaf.

ROOTSTOCK
The mass of roots some trees are grafted onto in order to control their size or protect from disease.

SAMARA
A winged fruit carrying a seed or seeds.

SAPLING
A young tree, typically less than 2 years old.

SCALE
A small, thin, often dry structure, such as protective leaves around a bud or a piece shed from a leaf or bark.

SHOOT
Young, new growth (stem), often a fresher green than other stems.

SINGLE FLOWER
A flower where the central part containing the pollen and nectar are usually visible.

SPP.
Abbreviation for species (plural).

STANDARD
A tree grown in a uniform shape with a single stem and distinct canopy.

STEM
Forming the skeleton of the plant, carrying nutrients between leaves and roots. In mature trees, this is the branches and twigs. Other stems, flowers, leaves, and fruit grow from it.

SUCKER
New stem growing from the base of the tree, or rootstock.

TAPROOT
A long, single root growing deep into the ground.

TRUNK
The main woody stem of a tree, usually covered in bark, from which its branches grow.

TWIG
Small branch.

UMBEL
A flat cluster of flowers.

WHIP
A slender, unbranched shoot or plant, typically a tree seedling.

Planting zones

When researching trees to plant, you will see a hardiness zone for each.
Below is a chart detailing temperatures and conditions for each hardiness
zone, which will give you an idea of how well a tree will do in your garden.

ZONE	EXTREME MINIMUM TEMPERATURE	STATES IN ZONE
1-2	−60°F to −40°F (−51.1°C to −40°C)	Alaska
3	−40°F to −30°F (−40°C to −34.4°C)	Alaska, Colorado, Idaho, Maine, Minnesota, Montana, New Hampshire, New York, North Dakota, Vermont, Wisconsin, Wyoming
4	−30°F to −20°F (−34.4°C to −28.9°C)	Alaska, Arizona, Colorado, Idaho, Iowa, Maine, Michigan, Minnesota, Montana, Nebraska, Nevada, New Hampshire, New Mexico, New York, North Dakota, Oregon, Utah, Vermont, Washington, Wisconsin, Wyoming
5	−20°F to −10°F (−28.9°C to −23.3°C)	Alaska, Arizona, California, Colorado, Connecticut, Rhode Island, Idaho, Illinois, Indiana, Iowa, Kansas, Maine, Maryland, Massachusetts, Michigan, Minnesota, Missouri, Montana, Nebraska, Nevada, New Hampshire, New Mexico, New York, North Carolina, Ohio, Oregon, Pennsylvania, Tennessee, Utah, Vermont, Virginia, Washington, West Virginia, Wisconsin, Wyoming
6	−10°F to 0°F (−23.3°C to −17.8°C)	Alaska, Arizona, California, Colorado, Connecticut, Rhode Island, Georgia, Idaho, Illinois, Indiana, Iowa, Kansas, Kentucky, Maine, Maryland, Massachusetts, Michigan, Missouri, Montana, Nevada, New Hampshire, New Jersey, New Mexico, New York, North Carolina, Ohio, Oklahoma, Oregon, Pennsylvania, Tennessee, Texas, Utah, Virginia, Washington, West Virginia, Wyoming
7	0°F to 10°F (−17.8°C to −12.2°C)	Alaska, Alabama, Arizona, Arkansas, California, Colorado, Connecticut, Rhode Island, Delaware, Georgia, Idaho, Illinois, Kansas, Kentucky, Maryland, Massachusetts, Mississippi, Missouri, Nevada, New Jersey, New Mexico, New York, North Carolina, Oklahoma, Oregon, Pennsylvania, South Carolina, Tennessee, Texas, Utah, Virginia, Washington, West Virginia
8	10°F to 20°F (−12.2°C to −6.7°C)	Alaska, Alabama, Arizona, Arkansas, California, Florida, Georgia, Louisiana, Maryland, Mississippi, Nevada, New Mexico, North Carolina, Oklahoma, Oregon, South Carolina, Tennessee, Texas, Utah, Virginia, Washington
9	20°F to 30°F (−6.7°C to −1.1°C)	Alabama, Arizona, California, Florida, Georgia, Hawaii, Louisiana, Mississippi, Nevada, New Mexico, Oregon, South Carolina, TexasUtah, Washington
10	30°F to 40°F (−1.1°C to 4.4°C)	Arizona, California, Florida, Hawaii, Louisiana, Nevada, Texas
11	40°F to 50°F (4.4°C to 10°C)	California, Florida, Hawaii
12-13	50°F to 70°F (10°C to 21.1°C)	Hawaii

Index

Acknowledgments

Author acknowledgments
Thanks to the brilliant team at DK for coming up with the idea for this book and for asking me to write it. Special shout-outs to Amy Slack and Ruth O'Rourke for helping put the book together and Jane Simmonds for painstakingly editing and cross-referencing it, including 50 tree profiles. Thanks also to Louise Brigenshaw and Mandy Earey for the design and to Vivienne Watton for getting the book out there.

Thanks to my wonderful agent Jane Turnbull, who is always there with an ear and a solution to a problem. Thanks to Chris Young for overseeing the whole thing and for his never-ending positivity and cheerfulness. I really appreciate you letting me be honest about climate change and for giving me a platform to write about what I love the most on this wonderful Earth of ours: trees, plants, and LIFE!

Thanks to Lucille Clerc for your amazing illustrations that transformed the book from a practical "how-to" to something you want to dive into and explore. Thanks to Kevin Martin, Head of the Arboretum at Kew, for your help on non-natives to grow in a changing climate, to Emma Crawforth at *BBC Gardeners' World Magazine* for always being on hand to answer random questions on tree IDs and varieties to grow. Thanks to Simon Maughan from the RHS for fact/sense-checking when I literally couldn't see the wood for the trees.

They were entirely useless in the creation of this book, but I would like to thank Emma and Tosca for being my girls. Researching and writing about climate change isn't fun, but they were always there to make me laugh. Tosca: stop growling at hedgehogs.

Illustrator acknowledgments
Thanks to the great team at DK and Kate Bradbury for their trust.

To my parents for teaching me to marvel at Nature everyday and to cultivate my own garden. Thanks to the wonderful man who taught me how to draw and to my ever-loving gardener mother—you two gave me inspiration for a lifetime. To my partner for his daily support—may our love grow as strong as the Major Oak.

I wish all you readers the joy of planting a tree: to watch it grow and gather with your loved ones under its welcoming foliage, to share its fruits, and to pass it on to the next generation.

Publisher acknowledgments
DK would like to thank Francesco Piscitelli for proofreading, Vanessa Bird for indexing, and John Tullock for US consulting.

ABOUT THE AUTHOR

Kate Bradbury is an award-winning author and journalist specializing in wildlife gardening. She edits the wildlife pages of *BBC Gardeners' World* magazine and regularly writes articles for *The Telegraph*, *The Guardian*, *RHS The Garden* magazine, and *BBC Wildlife* and *Wildlife Trust* magazines. She is the author of several books, including *The Wildlife Gardener*, memoir *The Bumblebee Flies Anyway* (both Bloomsbury), and *RHS How to Create a Wildlife Pond* (DK). She lives in Brighton, where her small but perfectly formed garden is home to ALL the wildlife, including hedgehogs, frogs and toads, house sparrows, starlings, and slow worms. She is ever hopeful of swifts. Her garden featured as part of the GardenWatch campaign for BBC Springwatch and Autumnwatch. Kate also appears on *BBC Gardeners' World*, where she demonstrates how to use garden plants to attract wildlife to small urban gardens like hers. She's a patron of Froglife and Bumblebee Conservation Trust and garden ambassador of Butterfly Conservation.

ABOUT THE ILLUSTRATOR

Lucille Clerc is a French graphic designer and illustrator based in London. She set up her studio after graduating from Central Saint Martins with an MA in Communication Design. She has illustrated a number of books and magazines and has also created works for the fashion industry and exhibition spaces. Much of her work is inspired by London's architecture and the relationship between nature and urbanization, with her compositions portraying her favorite places and exploring their past and present lives.

DK UK

Project Editor Amy Slack
Senior US Editor Kayla Dugger
Senior Designer Louise Brigenshaw
Jacket Designer Amy Cox
Jackets Coordinator Jasmin Lennie
Production Editor David Almond
Production Controller Rebecca Parton
Editorial Manager Ruth O'Rourke
Design Manager Marianne Markham
Art Director Maxine Pedliham
Publisher Katie Cowan

Illustrated by Lucille Clerc
Editor Jane Simmonds
Designer Mandy Earey
Consultant Gardening Publisher Chris Young

ROYAL HORTICULTURAL SOCIETY

Consultant Simon Maughan
Publisher Rae Spencer-Jones

First American Edition, 2022
Published in the United States by DK Publishing
1745 Broadway, 20th Floor, New York, NY 10019

Text copyright © Kate Bradbury 2022
Illustrations copyright © Lucille Clerc 2022
Illustrations on p148, p157, p159 and
p160 illustrated by Swindler & Swindler –
Folio Art © 2022 Dorling Kindersley Limited
Copyright © 2022 Dorling Kindersley Limited

DK, a Division of Penguin Random House LLC
22 23 24 25 26 10 9 8 7 6 5 4 3 2 1
001–321085–Sep/2022

A catalog record for this book
is available from the Library of Congress.
ISBN 978-0-7440-2693-1

Printed and bound in China

For the curious
www.dk.com

This book was made with Forest Stewardship Council ™ certified paper— one small step in DK's commitment to a sustainable future. For more information go to www.dk.com/our-green-pledge